SEX EXCURSIONIST

volume 2

Pattaya: 30 Days of Pain

NATHAN RENLY

Renly Publishing
www.nathanrenly.com

SEX EXCURSIONIST novels are published by

Renly Publishing

ISBN: 9781798482223

Contents

Transpacific dreaming

The most enjoyable night? Probably the blurry, drunken image of Ben's shit-eating grin while plowing the ass of the Soi 6 spinner as she braced herself against my shoulders, desperate to keep my dick from plopping out of her cunt. It certainly wasn't the goddess curled under my arm the last week, the image of every man's desires, ripping my heart and wallet away with her cold, savage touch.

Sitting in the cramped economy class of the eastbound A380, gliding above the Aleutians, my stomach churned like a bachelor jilted at the altar. "She's only a whore," I assured myself.

The world believes that men go to Pattaya for sex. Tens of thousands of young ladies offering their bodies to foreign men for the price of a nice dinner. For some of us who make the trip, we discover the offers far exceed sexual services. Emotions between myself and the girls I employ are often real. It's not the surgical style prostitution common in Western countries. Thai girls sell themselves to meet a foreigner, where age difference is not a deal-breaker, and the profession is merely a stepping stone.

Many men take advantage of this. Preying on the naïve girls' desires to find a husband, but themselves only interested in a fun getaway from Western life, and the feeling of being young again with a sexy lady. This is me. Paying for sex is fun, but the feeling of adoration is what I make the journey for. Though after THIS excursion, I wished I was merely a drunken sex-starved tourist, spending no more time with the girls than was necessary to climax. Simpler that way. Letting a Thai bargirl into your heart and wallet will ruin a vacation faster than a broken airplane engine.

The valium I availed myself of from the Thai pharmacy finally slowed my brain enough for the rehash of the prior month's events to ease and I drifted away with my head propped on the scrunched-up airline pillow.

Flying home was a smooth ride, the flight bound for Thailand a month earlier was anything but...

Noise on an airplane? I can stand it all... turbulence, crying babies, drunks, none of it bothers me anymore. If you get a kid kicking your chair, the best method of handling it is to turn around and play with her, try to grab her feet and tickle her, and be thankful you have such an easy distraction from the monotony of the flight. If given the opportunity, be sure to express to her mother sitting in the next seat how you are bound for Thailand to have sex with young ladies.

The westbound China Southern Triple-Seven rumbled over the eastern Pacific as I played catch-the-finger with the excitable Chinese girl. Shame her mother didn't speak a word of English but thrilled she was her daughter had a playmate. The kids will tire themselves out during the 14-hour flight, I didn't worry that I'd get my typical 5 or 6 power naps.

However, just as the kid had discovered some exhaustion and I had relaxed into my second in-flight movie, I felt the plane make a sharp right-hand turn. Checking the flight status and seeing the nose of the plane pointed back toward the states, I sighed at the bad luck. Hundreds of flights in life and I'd never had a flight turn around, why this one?

The other passengers finally got a clue themselves when the captain came on to explain in Chinese that we were in fact not heading west anymore. *No shit*.

When the cabin erupted in concerned voices, I asked the man beside me to explain. "Engine warning, we are landing Seattle." Oh great… Seattle. Wonder if I can find a 19-year-old to fuck me silly there for $50?

About Nathan Renly

Nathan Renly is a pen name. I've been an avid traveler all my life. In 2011, I began writing for a travel and outdoors blog, of course, never mentioning my scandalous night activities.

In 2015, I started keeping a journal about my interactions with sex workers, mostly in Southeast Asia and later turned them into my first book, Sex Excursionist: Angeles City.

My books are erotic, but also deal with the emotions I feel paying for the company of young, gorgeous women. Many of the non-fiction guides and blogs to red-light districts neglect to mention it, but I assure you, they are real… and painful as often as they are euphoric.

My other works:

Bangkok Layover: Nana plaza – A graphic look at a jet lagged stopover in Bangkok.
Sex Excursionist: Angeles City – The prelude to this book covering the favorite Philippine destination.
A Redhead on Soi 6 – A fictional short story of a young girl who becomes embroiled with a bargirl on Soi 6.

Nathanrenly.com

Pattaya Introduction

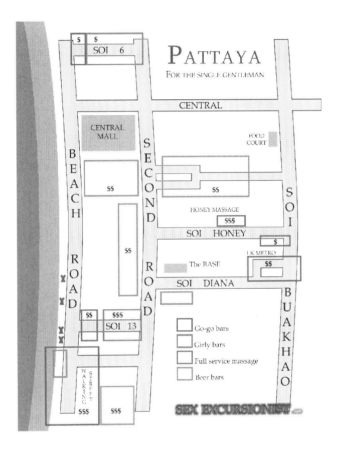

Pattaya is the capital of sex destinations. There is no better all-inclusive destination for the single male traveler. Thousands of girls starting at just 18-years-old await the lonely foreign gentleman in the bars, massage parlors, and streets of the ocean side thriving city of Pattaya, Thailand.

For a sex destination, Pattaya is massive. It may take some time for the new visitor to find the various sex districts scattered throughout the city. Each area has its own feel and often caters to a different sort of visitor. Walking Street, for example, caters to the bigger spender and less-frequent travelers, while Soi 6 caters to the more budget conscious visitor and men who want less foreplay.

Note: This guide is only meant to provide a quick introduction to Pattaya for readers. For more up-to-date travel information, as well as recommendations on hotels and bars, please visit SE's website.

Sexcursionist.com

Getting around

For the single male traveler interested in Pattaya's red-light districts, the area south of Central Road to Walking Street should be your focus. This area is within walking district to all of the city's red-light attractions and is organized by 3 streets that run north-south: Beach Road, Second Road, Soi Buakhao. It is about ¾ of a mile from Beach Road to Soi Buakhao.

The hotels and restaurants on Beach Road are nicer and more expensive. As you go inland, better deals can be found. Soi Buakhao is known for cheap guesthouses and budget outdoor eateries.

Motorbike taxis can zip you around or you can learn the system of songthaews (covered pickup trucks with benches that act as pseudo buses). The songthaews run south on Beach Road and north on Second Road for 10 baht.

A quick word on venues

Barfine: A fee paid to the bar so a lady may leave with the customer. Payment of the barfine implies sexual intercourse unless stated otherwise. Prices on this page stated in Thai Baht.

Pattaya Barfine Prices: The range for a sexual encounter in Pattaya is 1200 – 7000 depending on the girl, time agreed, and venue.

Go-go bars

These bars tend to be more upscale and are generally what travelers imagine of the sex trade in Thailand. A stage holds several girls who wait to be called down for drinks from patrons. Though mostly on Walking Street, some can be found in other areas. Dancers in these clubs might be picky with whom they barfine. (3k - 7k)

Girlie bars

These bars are sprinkled throughout the city, though they congregate on Soi 6. They may be plush comfortable venues or dive plastic-chair hole-in-the-walls. The girls will usually wear revealing attire and sit, waiting for customers. A stage in these bars is rare. Girls in these clubs are the easiest to barfine. (2k-5k)

Beer Bars

Outdoor venues with a long bar, usually in a square. These bars cater more to the drinkers and partygoers than sex-seeking tourists. Lady entertainers wearing anything from jean shorts and t-shirt to evening dresses await customers. Some will leave on a barfine while others stay in the bar all night entertaining. (2k - 5k)

Full-Service Massage Parlors

While the storefront may look like any professional massage parlor in the city, the ones with full service can usually be identified by plain-clothed masseuses. These can be found in the area of Soi Honey and Soi 13. (2k-5k)

Street Walkers

Concentrated on Beach Road near Walking Street, girls stand waiting to be approached by prospective customers. (1k-3k)

Pattaya Sex Districts

The streets of Pattaya can be confusing to the first-time visitor, who often finds himself at the mercy of the professional bargirl on Walking Street. However, for the more adventurous or budget-conscience traveler, other areas can provide a better service for a cheaper price.

Walking Street

Ah, Walking Street, Pattaya Thailand: a sex destination, a night scene, and a tourist attraction. The cobbled street under the shining Walking Street marque is shared by aging sex tourists, young backpackers, and bused-in tour groups.

The clubs here are mostly the go-go variety with the most beautiful girls in the country, some of which will be standing on the street hawking their respective club. With the quality of the clubs and girls, the prices are also inflated.

While the restaurants and open-air bars open for lunch, the go-go bars and nightclubs of Walking Street open around 8 pm and stay open until the early morning hours.

❖ Drinks 60 - 150
❖ Ladies drinks 200 - 400
❖ Barfine 3000 - 4000 Short time, 5000 - 7000 Long time

Soi 6

A little over a mile north on Beach Road from the Walking Street entrance is a sex pit you may not notice if you weren't looking for the standard round street sign with a 6.

Here, you can find a high concentration of girlie bars, or short-time bars, with convenient short-time rooms upstairs. The girls here are hardened prostitutes, less likely to be picky and also less likely to put up with bullshit.

The bars here open in the early afternoon and close shortly after nightfall, with the prime hours being between 4 pm and 7 pm. A stroll down the street at this time can often provide an experience of flirtation and laughter without even parting with your cash, as girls approach you to hawk their services.

❖ Drinks 60 - 120
❖ Ladies drinks 150 - 300
❖ Barfine 1500 – 3000 Short time, 3000 – 5000 Long time

Soi LK Metro

Named for the hotel which sits at one end of the alleyway that comprises Soi LK Metro, visitors will find a more laid-back and less-pretentious feeling in the go-go bars.

The bars here are simple with a stage in the middle and booths aligning the walls. The girls will be friendlier and more eager to make money than their Walking Street counterparts and less-hardened then those on Soi 6. I've always enjoyed my barfines from LK Metro.

The bars here open in the late afternoon and stay open until around midnight.

❖ Drinks 80 - 150
❖ Ladies drinks 200 - 350
❖ Barfine 2500 – 3000 Short time, 3000 – 5000 Long time

Soi Honey

Named for Honey Body Massage sitting prominently mid-street, Soi Honey is for those seeking quick relief. Don't expect to need to wine and dine your short-time lady, nor should you expect to be turned down.

In Honey Massage, girls are arranged around a middle seating area and flooded with lights so you can thoroughly judge their assets. In the room, expect a pampered service, body-to-body rubdown, and safe sex.

On the street, toward the intersection with Soi Buakhao are the less-frills versions of full-service massage. Here you can find some of the cheapest quick fucks in the city... and no, not much of a massage, if any.

- ❖ Honey Massage 2500 - 4000
- ❖ Street Stalls 1200 - 2000

Soi 13

You might wander down Soi 13 on an early trip to Pattaya as you explore the area around Walking Street. The street takes a bit from all styles of sexual venues with go-go bars, girlie bars, and full-service massage on offer.

The feel of Soi 13 is a bit of a cross between LK Metro and Soi 6 with career-oriented girls out to suck the life out of the naïve visitor as well as those girls who may be more relaxed and enjoy sitting around drinking beer.

Prices can be somewhat high here due to its proximity to Walking Street and the high-end hotels.

- ❖ Drinks 150 - 350
- ❖ Ladies drinks 200 - 350
- ❖ Barfine 2500 – 3000 Short time, 3000 – 5000 Long time
- ❖ Full-service massage 2000 - 3000

Beach Road Walkers

Why not go directly to the source? Skip the bars and massage parlors all-together? It's an easy option and girls line Beach Road stretching away from Walking Street at all hours of the day.

While Pattaya is generally safe for the sex-connoisseur, if you are looking for trouble with a girl, this is where you'll find it. Since you can never be sure where to find her again, be mindful of theft, and be sure to use a condom.

❖ Negotiated fee 1000 – 2500

1

Stench on Soi 13

No, this isn't a story about Seattle. My 12-hour unplanned layover there went smoothly, though I couldn't manage more than a $200 voucher toward a future flight... the downside of buying trans-pacific rock-bottom tickets from Chinese airlines. There were no 19-year-old's in the bar next to the hotel willing to sell sexual services either, in fact, I couldn't even find a 40-year-old desperate hag. I didn't search much though, as I rarely do in America. Why waste my money in a country where sex is considered a sin and I'm looked down on for engaging in it with anyone other than a wife of 20 years? It was an airport hotel and more boob-tube for me, awaiting my journey to a paradise where sex is easy and cheap, and I'm as appreciated for purchasing it as I appreciate the lovely ladies who are willing to offer it. This is a story about Pattaya, Thailand, the world's sex capital for lonely men of all ages.

And lonely man I am. Relationships are hard for me. I dream of sex all day, finding any interaction that doesn't involve sex a waste of time. Yet, I fall in love easily, especially if the sex is good. It never lasts, as there is a constant thought wiggling around in my mind that asks, "What if there is something better out there?" The incessant seeking of more satisfying sex with a more desirable woman forces me to expand my options out of my home country and far below my age of 49.

40 hours after the first engine problem in my lifetime of travels, my plane touched down in Bangkok on a sunny February afternoon. The muted excitement of my fellow Chinese travelers did little to calm me. I was tired of sitting on a plane, in an airport, or a budget hotel. I should have been balls deep in a few Thai spinners by now. Patience with traveling and buying pussy has always been my strongpoint, but this sort of delay and the terror of a jet experiencing an engine problem stressed me into impatience... and breaking some of my rules. Such as...

Learn to take buses, trains, and songthaews[1].

Getting from Bangkok to Pattaya is easy. There is no need to book a car, simply take the moving pathways from the arrival terminal to the lowest floor and look out the windows for rows of buses. Mumble "pah TIE ya"[2] to a Thai worker and a finger will go in the air. The cost at the time of this writing was 120 baht ($4 US). Though the bus doesn't go to Pattaya beach, you can get dropped off on Sukhumvit road and Central road, then grabbing a songthaew or motorbike taxi (60 baht) to your hotel.

---

[1] Songthaews are pickup trucks redesigned with a top and inward facing seats for ferrying travelers along a specific route, basically a cheap bus.

[2] Thais pronounce it more like "pa tay YA" though no matter how hard I try to say it like them, I'm never understood, yet saying it like a foreigner seems to always be understood.

Get a Thai sim card at the airport.

Prior to boarding the bus, stop by one of the many mobile phone kiosks such as *AIS* or *True move*. Hopefully, you've already removed your American sim card or if you're really good, moved it to the second sim card slot in your phone and turned off mobile data. Even the best Western plans will not save you money over a Thai prepaid sim card, and besides, you need a local Thai number for the girls. If you are in a rush like I was, you can get a sim card on any street in Pattaya, but you'll probably want to flip through online dating sites like Tinder on the 3-hour drive.

As for me, I bypassed the mobile phone stalls, stopped at the currency exchange, and raced straight out the arrival terminal toward the waiting yellow cabs, ignoring the white-shirted ride hawkers offering rides to Pattaya. 2,700 baht would be the price, over 10x more than public transport, and likely less than an hour of time saved. I justified it with my $200 flight voucher. I suppose I should give myself a break. I was tired and desperately wanted to get my dick inside a Thai girl, something I'd waited and dreamed of for a year. The vacation had not started off the same as in my dreams back home. In those dreams, I'd gotten a full 6 hours of sleep on the plane and arrived in Bangkok ready but relaxed, flipped through the pages of waiting freelancers on Tinder during the smooth bus ride, and had one waiting for me when I arrived.

Instead, when I arrived at my condo building, I dumped my bags with security and raced out into the failing evening light of Pattaya with hardly a care for my stench of travel and exhaustion in my body, and only a vague idea of the party I was looking for.

Adrenaline pushed me forward as I stepped onto Second Road and lost myself in the slow crawl of pedestrian traffic consisting of men from all countries and the occasional Thai girl carefully stepping over the cracked sidewalks and around the oddly placed telephone poles. The rumble and horns of traffic on Second Road moved the opposite way slower than the foot traffic on the other side, with songthaews mingling with taxis and scooters slipping through any available space.

I glanced at the solemn faces of male travelers like myself. Most of them acted like they were ashamed to be out, avoiding eye contact as if not wanting to be noticed, going about their business bound for a tavern and a mug of beer or the cheap bed of a short time hotel. I suspected I looked the same, I had a mission and it didn't concern them.

Less than a hundred steps and I felt the trickle of sweat on my legs under the comfortable gym pants I wore on the plane. The tropical heat of Pattaya was sapping what energy I had left. I thought for a moment that sleep and a shower would be a better idea and the girls of Pattaya could wait, but the compulsion to engage in the sexual encounter I'd waited so long for won over and I continued my ramble toward the first red-light spot that popped in my head: Soi 13.

Soi 13 is actually 4 streets (13/1, 13/2...) of girlie bars and massage parlors mingled with restaurants and hotels spanning between Beach Road and Second Road. Because of its proximity to Walking Street, it gets its share of novice travelers and therefore its inflated prices. Had I been in my right mind, I would have gone the opposite direction toward the budget short time spots such as Soi Honey or Soi 6. Despite that, Soi 13 would be a good pick for quickly getting to business with a full-service girl of above average beauty.

On the 3rd Soi 13, I poked my head around the open-air bar on the corner and caught sight of what I was looking for. Large capital-letter massage signs extended into the street. I attempted to appear as if just out for a stroll as I passed the bar of white-faced men sitting stoically downing their beers. I wasn't fooling any of them though. I'm sure they'd made the solo walk down the street to fish a girl out many times. Were they tourists or expats? Who knows, it can be difficult to tell the regular visitors from the expats. Often regular visitors become expats.

I felt their eyes on my back as my world changed from the businesslike state of Second Road to the sex-on-offer environment of Soi 13. Finally, my eyes fell upon that which I desired – sex-workers. The one-lane street ran between various bars and massage parlors, all of which had young ladies sitting out front, their eyes trained on the street as if I was walking through a gauntlet of salesladies. There would be no escaping them, no sneaking around, they knew when perverts approached.

"Ma-sage!" came the familiar call in a high-pitched voice. My mood improved, forgetting the bar of judgmental pricks and my insecurities, when a young Thai lady in a massage uniform called to me from the left side. She sat amongst a dozen of her friends, all wearing the same orange skirt and white shirt. Across the street, in front of the lone go-go bar, an attractive young girl in an evening dress turned toward me, waiting for my decision. I wanted to run to her. She was the most beautiful sight. My stomach fluttered, my groin tingled, and a primitive instinct arose to rush to her. *Would she mate with me?*

As I kept right on the street, more girls called from the group of masseuses on the left side, as if they could persuade me their way. I began to feel uneasy again, as I neared the starlet. A go-go bar would require a barfine, maybe a drink as well, and a wait while she changed clothes if she'd even go with me. The massage parlor on the left was the uniformed variety, not the full-service variety. As much as I wanted to do my deed right here, right now, I knew I must press on, to find the quick short-time experience I needed so I could pass out after the grueling travel.

I grinned to both sides of the street as if to say, "Ha, I know you want me, but you can't have me." Then, I continued.

Another uniformed massage parlor, an open-air bar, a girlie bar, all of them with hawkers beckoning me inside. Urging me to spend money on drinks. No, I wanted sex, and fast. I would know the true prostitutes when I saw them.

Ahead of me, another man falling prey to the screams and coercions of the various door girls had a tiny arm wrapped around his waist as he pushed forward. She was barely half his height, with black heels supporting skinny brown legs, a hardly visible pair of blue jean shorts, and a black tank top. Her black hair swayed with her hips as she kept pace with the man urging him to follow her. As I moved in closer, I was again taken by butterflies. She was small and sexy, and she was out to get fucked.

To the right, a group of plain-clothed girls sat in front of "Message Macca," laughing and encouraging her as if it was her turn to get a customer. A plain-clothed massage parlor was perfect, she was perfect, and as our gazes locked and I approached, she understood.

"Hey hon - eee, are you ready?" she asked in a thick accent.

The girls were having some kind of contest on how quickly she could pick up a customer, as they egged her on. I was ready the moment she put her arm around my waist. I could have dropped down on the street and fucked the hell out of her right there. As if to help seal the deal, she pressed her tight body against mine, wrapped the other arm around me, pulled me close and stared seductively. Her face was classic Thai — flat with a small nose and small mouth, cute but probably pushing 30. An experienced sex-worker for certain, exactly what I needed.

I babbled something about being ready. The culture shock of simply being there was nothing compared to the shock of speaking to a Thai girl. It wasn't the first time, but it takes adjustment. I could speak John-to-sex-worker talk though. I wrapped my arms around the little thing and pulled her close, causing an explosion of hormones. I had not felt the touch of a woman in months. I may have been shaking as we walked inside the massage parlor.

Or more accurate, the sex shop. The lobby was a small tiled room with a simple wood counter where an older lady sat waiting for payment. Crusty couches lined each wall, and a few pairs of flip-flops lay pushed against the outer glass.

Sleep and shower first, then sex.

"Hey, shoes!" she barked at me. I had walked right into the building with my running shoes on, my normal footwear for planes, forgetting the Thai custom of leaving your shoes at the door. I sat and removed them, an explosion of my own stench escaping. *Oh, damn, I might need a shower.*

I stepped carefully across the clean tile floor, my sweaty, oily feet shifting with each slimy contact. I felt more uneasiness, wanting to flee from the strange world and strange customs, my aging body screaming, "Something is wrong here, abort! Abort!" But my eyes guided me onward to my petite darling waiting at the counter, with a look of disinterest but also of total acceptance.

An hour of oil massage at 300 baht. Standard. The house gets their cut.

"I need a shower," I said.

"It's ok, don't worry," my masseuse said, as she grabbed my hand and led me to a set of stairs behind the counter. *Well, I offered.*

The skinny stairs were made of the same tile as the floor below and my feet seemed resistant to drying off in the tropical air. I lumbered up, feeling as if I'd slip off every step, using the knee-high handhold to steady myself with one hand and disallowing her to run up with my other. She probably thought she was helping, but her tugs did little, like a child trying to drag a toy chest up a stairway.

Entering the dark massage room put me at ease, though I'd suspect would startle the novice Pattaya visitor. The tile floor continued, and in a room, the size of the lobby, was five old massage beds arranged haphazardly around. On the left wall was a drawn curtain in the shape of a sixth bed with a pair of dark female feet visible. There was a musty smell, of old linens and sweat which the single wall-mounted air conditioner did little to disperse.

"Here," my massage girl whispered. She pulled the curtains around a bed close to the in-progress massage. I couldn't help but think a table on the other side would be a better choice. Another cultural difference I'd presume. Westerners love their space, Thais never have it, so they never think of it. I should have said something and would have had my brain been in a better state. Sleep and shower first, then sex.

It was an impersonal space for sex. It's more like what a cheap therapeutic massage parlor would offer. But with the curtains drawn and the two of us enclosed, my apprehensions vanished and blood began rushing to my crotch. All these months, and all the travel troubles, but here I was about to engage in a man's duties with a desirable young lady, leave the curtains open for I all care.

"Clothes here," she whispered, patting the small space at the head of the table beside the pillow. I waited for her to leave, as I'm accustomed to, but she stood there, a grin popping up as she realized my shyness in stripping naked. Well, if I had any idea this wasn't a full-service massage parlor, they were gone now. I pulled my clothes off and my erect penis slapped into view.

"Wow, so big!" she said.

Those words. A week or so into a sex vacation, they mean little to me, about as truthful as "handsome." But my self-confidence was at a low-point before this day and the wave of pride came with euphoria. Instinctively, I moved toward her reaching out my arms.

She laughed.

She blocked my grope.

"Massage first, honey."

I laid face-first on the table, sex on my brain, my eyes never leaving her tiny legs. *How long until they'd be wrapped around me?*

I laid the side of my face on the pillow, no comfortable hole on this table, it was just a pillow. *Wait, this is a full-service massage!* I reached a hand to my groin to point my dick between my legs, giving her more than my legs to massage. The teasing sensation of fingertips was almost as enjoyable as the sex.

As my hand contacted my pubic hair, I was reminded of the coat of sweat and oil on my body. Thoughts raced through my head. Had she already noticed my B.O.? Did she care? Oh, whatever, it's Thailand.

So little had been said between her and me. I doubted she spoke much English besides the phrases that were necessary to do her work. After she unfolded a small towel that barely draped over my ass, she disappeared outside the curtain. What little noise her and I had been making left and the noise from the next bed became noticeable.

A man was moaning, the unmistakable sound of sexual pleasure. He sounded Asian, perhaps Japanese, which would explain the restrained effort, like he didn't want to be heard. Besides his slow, shy whimpers, there was no other sound. No bed moving, no female voice. He must have been receiving a blowjob, perhaps this whole time? The masseuse could be standing up, I surmised since we didn't hear any discussion since I saw her feet from outside the curtain. What a distraction it must have been when we entered! I silently rooted for the man, to cum in her throat, and get some relief.

I heard my masseuse return, still without a word. A squirt from a bottle and the sound of her hands rubbing together. Finally, the intimate contact I was craving. Her hands rubbed my shoulders like the amateur hands of a high school girlfriend. Another squirt and her hands moved down my back. No more sounds from next door, the physical tension from the days of traveling were easing, but the tension from the anticipation of what was next took its place. As her hands moved over the top of my buttocks, I moaned, much louder than our friend, though I'd forgotten about him.

She worked her hands around my back, doing a massage she'd probably taught herself over the years, a routine that didn't tire her, but still attempted to satisfy her customer. If it were a professional massage, I'd feel ripped off, but I was more interested with how often she'd touch my butt. Don't get that in a professional massage. *It wasn't as much as I'd have preferred*.

The towel across my butt never came off as she moved to my legs. Probably a good thing. I could sniff my underarms, no doubt my bare ass could be smelt by the couple on the next bed. But the towel still in place suggested she wouldn't do a lot of flirting with that area, a total let down in my book. Her hands worked around my legs, teasing but never contacting my protruding member. With each motion of her hand northward, my hopes would raise but were dashed as she moved back to my calves. I sighed and relaxed, my raging hard-on pressing against the hard table getting some respite.

Next door, the man had finally mounted her, or perhaps she'd mounted him, who knows, but the additions of soft moans of a Thai lady and the subtle rattling of a wooden massage table distracted me of the happenings between my legs. The man's voice was silent, nothing. That wouldn't be me later, whether we were alone or not. It seemed even my masseuse was drawn to listening to the coitus, as her hands were now just squeezing a single calf.

"Turnover please." The request in my ear startled me and came barely ten minutes from when the massage started, but was welcomed nonetheless, I wasn't there for a massage. The Thai lady next door was still going at it when I lifted myself and flipped over, the towel falling to the floor and my semi-erect penis coming into view. A whiff of odor as well. She didn't seem to notice.

She reached down to pick up the towel, but to my surprise only placed it on the table between my legs. *Ah, she'd need it later*. She climbed the table and sat over my quads, my crotch in easy reach. For the first time, I heard a moan from the man, this time uninhibited.

Her face shined, a big smile with crooked teeth as she leered at me. Her face turned seductive as her hands found my crotch, one rubbing my balls, and the other yanking my dick into full erection.

"Oh yes, honey," she whispered.

Her face turned to my crotch for a moment, and I could see her right nostril snarl, and I was certain she'd caught a whiff of my stink. *Bet now you wish you hadn't rushed me up here.*

Normally, I'd be embarrassed to the point of performance issues but not this day. This day I could have fucked a chubby whore who smelled worse than me. So long as this sweet girl would have me, my dick wasn't going to let me down.

As the man's moans became louder and he approached climax, she stroked me, and she smiled as if being entertained by the noise next to us, or perhaps she was using it as a selling tactic.

I relaxed and pulled my hands behind my head to watch her. The moment my armpits exposed to the room, the stroking stopped and her face drooped. *Oops.*

I returned my arms to my side and laughed. No shame in me at all, but no need to torture the poor girl.

She mumbled something incoherent. It was supposed to be English, probably the beginnings of negotiation.

The man's moan as he climaxed was charming, a gentleman relieving himself of the stress of the cruel world outside. The noise from the table never increased but kept the same soft rattle. First, the ecstatic explosion of the first blast and then the pained labor of full release as the table rustle died down and the Thai voice quietly asked, "Ok, sir?"

There I was, laying on my back in the stench of travel halfway around the world waiting for my turn to release the stress of my first-world life, I doubt much different from the Asian man who went first. For me, the experience was dulled, I'd made the trip many times. But no longer dulled was my masculinity. I was a different man there, no longer restrained attempting to conform to a civilized world. I could smile and laugh about sex and the sounds a total stranger made when performing it. And more importantly, I could fuck this beautiful woman for no other reason than being attracted to her, without a care in the world. No one would judge me here, and even if they did, I'd go home in a month and never see them again.

I leaned up and grabbed her, my hands running over the tight sides of her torso and up her back. My attempt for a kiss was returned carefully, her lips blocking any attempt to get my tongue into her mouth. As my hands moved up the front of her tight shirt, she leaned back and assisted by pulling it up. Her small mounds appeared in the dim light, smooth brown skin, small erect nipples. I played with them as if they were the first I'd ever touched.

When dealing with Thai prostitutes, start the negotiation with a low price, and always know the going rate.

"What you want?" she asked. *Oh right, there's always the money part.*

"You... Uh... Everything..." *Way to go, rook.*

Her coy demeanor turned to business.

"Fie tao zand, for eh re ting."

The first encounters of my sex vacations are often like this, negotiating with a prostitute only a few minutes into the encounter after she's tickled my balls and gotten my brain thinking not much else than making babies. It's a miracle I wasn't drunk yet. Though it's hard to get a good price when they can sense your desire, when dealing with Thai prostitutes, start the negotiation with a low price, and always know the going rate.

"Isn't it more like three thousand?" I asked.

"O kee, honey!" she yelled. "Four! But you so lucky!"

"Okay," I said. *She would have taken two.*

"You ha condom?" she asked.

Blank look.

"No."

"Oh, wait honey."

She released my cock, bounced off the bed, and ducked out the curtain.

After a few seconds, I heard her conversing in Thai to another girl, maybe the girl servicing the Asian man next to me. Their voices whispered, but they spoke fast, like coworkers relaying the days shift to each other. *"Handsome white guy?" "Big dick in there?"* I imagined her being asked.

Their voices increased as they talked over each other and I recognized a cheer in my masseuse's voice, until they both broke into laughter, and then suppressed it. As she returned, a hand reached through the opening.

The curtain rustled as she continued her conversation, not paying much attention to how much of me was exposed. As she took a step back, the curtain draped over her shoulder creating a low gap through which I could see the other masseuse, who was even more attractive than mine wearing a loose t-shirt and jean shorts. Her eyes darted to my naked body for a moment and then returned to her friend as if she'd seen nothing of interest.

The conversation continued as I lay there, my dick shriveling up with every screeched Thai word. Too shy to stroke it and too nervous to interrupt them, I lay waiting, pondering their topic. I suppose from their point of view, they are just going about their work, taking the time to catch each other up when they both had reason to step away. For me, it was supposed to be a sensual moment of ecstasy, for her... monotony.

"Oh, thank you, thank you," I heard the Asian man say. *Hey, how about that curtain now?*

"It's ok, sir," the other masseuse said as their Thai conversation stopped.

"She vewy nice," said my masseuse.

The Asian man stepped into view to shake his girl's hand. His head turned to me and then snapped back, before my curtain was pulled and my world shrank again to just her and me. *Well, if that doesn't kill your libido, what does?*

"Sowy honey."

She threw a silver wrapper between my legs and proceeded with her disrobing. A mechanical process, the way you'd expect a girl to undress in private. As for me, I sat up on my elbows and stared. For a girl of her size, she had a great figure. Firm breasts with pointy nipples on a skinny tight body. Her ass was a bit flat, like most Asians, especially at her age, but the lower cheek had a plumpness sitting over her skinny legs. The dark skin I'd seen up until now ceded to a defined tan line and a creamy natural skin.

"Oh, so big!" she said.

She leaned her belly against the table and took my limp dick and balls with both hands. *Big?*

She pulled on me, urging me into action as if she had a line of customers outside. I was busy contemplating the "big" statement. Surely, she says that to everyone, does that really work on guys? Well, maybe she's used to Asian customers, maybe I really am big even without a hard-on. Yes, that must be it, she knows I'll be too big for her after I get hard. *And with those thoughts, my dick grew.*

"Oh, yes, come on, honey," she said.

"Blowjob?" I asked.

"Oh, you want smoke[3]?" she asked.

"Right, smoke," I said.

"O kee."

She leaned forward, frowned, and then leaned back. If she had a problem with anything, I'd be happy to renegotiate the price we'd agreed upon.

Perhaps she was simply not tall enough to smoke while standing. She climbed on the table between my legs and dropped to her knees, never looking me in the eye, her

---

[3] Smoke – A Blowjob. Like she's smoking a cigarette.

intent staying on my crotch, and her face never showing a positive expression. Was it the stench or did she simply not like this part of her job?

With both hands she pushed my pubic hair down carefully, redoing the motion to get as much out of the way as she could. Maybe that helped with the odor as well. By now, regardless of the dispassionate service, my dick had grown, while I waited for the tiny person to service me. I put my hands behind my head and relaxed. *Whew, that stinks, ah well, fuck it.*

Then finally, after all these long months, and a grueling journey, I had what I sought, a woman's mouth around the head of my penis. Well... at least lips around the head. And only the head. It was like a ring of dry skin lurching back and forth over the tip. No tongue, no saliva, might as well have been a finger and thumb. *I guess that's how you smoke a cigarette.*

I waited a moment to see if her performance increased, but while I may have been right off the plane, I was far from a total newb when it came to sex workers. I put my hand on the top of her head and urged her downward. Her head stopped, her eyes glared at me, and then she submitted to my suggestion. *No, you're not getting off that easy.*

Still with her hands mashing my pubic hair, I felt her tongue contact the underside of my head. There was not a lot of room in that mouth, keeping my dick dry would be impossible. Once I had a good motion going, I removed my hand. She continued the motion for a few seconds before easing back to her original range. I put my hand back on her head until she got the idea. While she resisted, I suspect she knew better than to fight me before I'd given her the high price she demanded. She's lucky I didn't try to jam it down her throat.

About two minutes in, a bit of saliva dripped down my shaft and I rested my hands behind my head again to watch, she learned fast. Her little body pumped up and down as she worked me in her mouth, her eyes closed, and her black hair hanging around her ears. *Oh so big*, she had said and from this angle, I looked monstrous, her little head latched onto the end of my dick like a school girl sucking on the end of a long Popsicle. *Woh, where did that come from?*

I slapped myself. "Ok, that's good," I said.

She lifted up. Her face looked pained from the effort. I've had girls choke on my dick who looked less frazzled. How did I manage to find this snob of a whore as my first encounter? Oh, yeah, I didn't take the time to look around, that's how.

She tore open the condom and rolled it over me, again pressing down my pubic hair with each motion, which was now a mat of spit and bush. I'd assume she was getting used to my stench, I know I was.

"Doggy-style?" she asked.

If there is an English phrase that Thai girls say perfectly, it's "doggy-style."

I sighed.

"No," I said. "Lay down."

We flipped and she laid down and dutifully opened her legs, exposing a tiny bald pussy with tight lips and a thin clit. The thoughts of fucking a child came to me, but I looked at her 30-year-old face and brushed those thoughts away.

I mounted her as she leaned up to help guide me in. The tip of my covered dick contacted her pussy and didn't get anywhere.

"Oh, so big," she said. *Yea, you know it.*

She massaged her clit in a circular motion and slipped one finger inside her. Her normal routine I suspect. Then she grabbed me and pulled. My dick slid in almost as if I were fucking a chubby American girl. Probably with the aid of used lubricant from an earlier encounter.

Well, I'd better see if I can find the bottom of her. I began to pound her. Her nose snarled and she lay back and turned her head. I seemed to have plenty of room inside, I should go harder.

"Oh come here, honey," she said.

She pulled on my neck, wanting me to get off my hands and lay on her, obviously so I'd have less leverage. That didn't really seem fun to me. I resisted her and kept pounding.

"My God!" she yelled.

She leaned up and wrapped her arms around my neck. Her goal was to ease the assault, but the feel of her body distracted me and I dutifully followed her command. She's lucky it was my first encounter of the trip. For 4,000 baht, I should have been able to pound her and stick a finger up her ass at the same time… twice.

My body perspired as I lay my torso against hers. I wrapped an arm around the back of her neck exposing my armpit to her face, which she recoiled from. With the other hand, I pinched her nipple. Then I pushed my dick up her pussy forcing her shoulders against my elbow. Though she seemed a little put off by my smell, the new position satisfied her. She closed her eyes and waited for me to finish.

A bead of sweat rolled down my cheek and onto my chin, ready to drop on my lover at any moment. I could catch it, but it would require letting go of her nipple. It landed on her forehead. She wiped it away without a change of expression, just part of the job.

I collapsed on my other elbow, bringing our bodies closer together. She squirmed under my weight as I kept prodding her. The silky feeling of her stomach and tits running across my damp beer belly... ah, *bliss.*

I buried my face in her neck and hair as my primitive desire urged me closer to her. Then I caught a new odor. It wasn't me this time. A day's work rounding up customers in the sun and servicing them inside is bound to make a girl stink. Did she ever take a shower in between? Perhaps that's why she didn't rush me to a shower. Does this place even have a shower?

Two smelly people romping it on a cheap wooden table surrounded by a faded white curtain. Well, not the best start to a sex vacation, but it worked for me. And…

Three-minute man. Hey, maybe you could do better with a sexy spinner for your first fuck in months, but I was done, much to her pleasure. She scrambled off the bed, dressed, and helped remove the condom with some tissue. 30 minutes into my one-hour massage and I was handing her the outrageous amount of 4,000 baht, and mimicking her Thai thank you, both hands in front of the chest with a "Kop Kun Kop," and I was on my way back to the condo.

Walking past the same guys at the bar on the corner, this time I waved and smiled. Some returned a head nod, most ignored me.

It wasn't the greatest pay-for-play sexual experience in my life. I suppose it wasn't the worst either, though, on the value scale, it had to have been far down there. Maybe the haggard old white woman in the Nevada brothel was worse.

I didn't concern myself with it though, I was in Pattaya, and only good things were to come. *Or so I thought...*

For this trip, I chose to stay a week longer than my usual 3 weeks and booked an AirBnB condominium for the month of February. There are a few advantages to booking a condo with the number one being cost. I found a nice clean condo at the BASE which sits on Second Road next to Soi Honey for $650 including utilities. While it's difficult to compare condos to hotel rooms since condos come with separate sitting areas and a kitchen, I'd expect to spend $60 per day for a hotel room of similar build and furniture. Additionally, having a refrigerator, stove, and microwave allows me to cook some of my meals saving even more on my food bill.

There are some hefty disadvantages to booking a condo for the whole trip. I'd say the number one disadvantage is not having daily maid service. Let's be real, being on a sex trip means bed linens need to be changed often, sometimes daily, and the condo will quickly grow a collection of black hairs if not swept. Being on a vacation, I loathe cleaning myself and contracting a regular maid service will close the gap of the cost difference of a hotel. Having a girl clean is one option, many will offer, but then you are blurring the line between customer and boyfriend and as a boyfriend comes the expectation of monogamy during the trip.

There is also less security in a condo. Hotels in sex destinations attempt to protect both the customer and the sex worker. In Pattaya, a local girl visiting your hotel room must leave an ID at the desk. This is a significant advantage to the customer making theft more difficult. It also protects the girl from a predator knowing there will be a record of the girl's whereabouts. There's not really anyone watching in a condo building. My landlord at least installed a safe, though, and since I rarely get drunk and pass out, there is not much a girl could take advantage of me for.

It was 7 pm when I received the keys to my condo, quickly washed the stench away, and passed out.

2

Honey Massage and a Post-Op

Jetlag can cause some unique experiences, especially on a sex vacation. I've learned to not fight it. I sleep when I know my body wants to sleep while adjusting it slowly. It's a vacation and my enjoyment is largely dependent on how good I feel.

I go on these trips for the go-go bars. I find pleasurable the experience of perusing a line-up of girls and enjoying the company of those I choose for drinks until I find one that I connect with and take her out for the night or just home to fuck. Often the girls in the clubs are not hardened hookers, or less so than other sex workers such as at massage parlors or on the street whose aim is to go through as many customers as possible. Go-go girls are selling a lengthier service that includes more than sex and often they are selling themselves to meet a foreigner for marriage so, during the encounter, there may be some genuine interest. Age isn't a big deal in Thailand. Though go-go bargirls are rarely over 23, less than half my age, the interactions are usually no different than if I was their own age.

During the first several days in Pattaya, I found myself exhausted around 6 pm and by 8 pm, miserable to continue fighting sleep. Then I was sleeping until 4 am or so, with a groggy rise so that I didn't get moving until 5 am or 6 am[4]. I

---

[4] On Jet Lag: This is typical for the average traveler from America who doesn't fight the jet lag. Travelers who

felt great in the mornings and afternoon having received such a long natural sleep, but I was also sleeping through the hours of all the go-go bars. I knew this sleep schedule wouldn't last long, as I was staying up later and sleeping later every night. I simply needed to tide myself over with girls from other venues.

It seemed obvious what I would do on my first full day: A Soapy! A Soapy Massage is almost strictly a Thai experience. I've never found them anywhere else in the world, and I'd only experienced it once in Bangkok on my only visit there. I enjoyed it in Bangkok, though I found it a little expensive.

Soi Honey, named for Honey Body Massage, which is the most noticeable attraction on the street, was less than a minute walk from my condo. If the whole procedure of a full-service massage wasn't so impersonal, I'd likely avail myself of it quite often during the trip, but I feel it's just a place to bust a nut and only slightly more enjoyable than jerking off. In fact, if I could have the bath and body massage by itself for half the price, it may seem like a better value.

The line-up area of Honey Massage was lacking the glass separation of girls and customers. There were two areas with girls on each side and some luxurious furniture in the middle. The girls were blasted with spotlights with the middle customer area somewhat darkened. A cute skinny

---

fight it, and urge themselves into the bars through the evening hours will find themselves unable to get a full night's rest. It's the same as staying up all night and going to bed at noon. The body doesn't want to sleep then, it thinks it's time to be awake.

woman in her late twenties approached me as I entered. She was wearing a sophisticated pantsuit and sported a corporate salesperson smile.

"Hello, is this your first time?" she asked. I'm sure that was an easy assumption for her as she was likely there every day.

My first thought was, "Can I have you?" I didn't bother with actually asking the question though, didn't think she'd want to give up her cushy mama-san job. There is just something about pantsuits that gets me every time.

I'm not experienced with the bathtub scene. The "pick a girl and go fuck" routine never really appeals to me. How am I supposed to get excited about a girl I haven't spoken a single word to or even shaken the hand of? I sat down to have a beer and try to work it out.

It was obvious that one side was the cheap side and another side was the expensive side. The price difference was only 500 baht (2,500 and 3,000), so I knew I would be getting a girl from the more expensive side. After sitting for a few minutes, the pantsuit made her way back over to help me.

"What do you like? Slim?" she asked. I guess there were a lot of bigger girls on the cheaper side and I wasn't looking much in that direction. I told her yes, that I liked slim.

"She's new and very young, but she's more, 3,800 baht," she said pointing to a young girl on the end of the expensive side.

"Pass." I guess she thought I was into the young ones. I had noticed her sitting there but though young wasn't more attractive than some of the other girls.

"Ok, there are slim girls…" and she began to point out several girls by number, many of which I'd already picked out myself.

I let the pantsuit walk away and tried to determine a way I would decide on a girl. There really isn't a good system to use that I've found. Sometimes I'd simply choose the girl that seems the most attractive and other times I'd choose a girl making eye contact. Maybe, I'd choose a girl that seemed eager to work, which I could easily judge by whoever was not playing with their phone. The latter strategy would have made it very easy as only one was not playing with her phone. In fact, she was straight out staring me down. Her eyes were locked to mine and every time I would look at her, which was hard not to do because of her gaze, she would smile. I felt like I was being stalked… I couldn't pick her, it would have been as if it wasn't even my decision.

After narrowing the choices down to girls wearing two-piece outfits so I could verify their midsection had no stretch marks, I finally picked the only girl that would look up occasionally and smile at me, Number 42. She struck me as a career soapy massage girl. She was completely at ease with the interaction and seemed to know she was going to be picked. I told the pantsuit who called out her number and robotically motioned me towards the side of the room where the cashier was. Number 42 joined me there.

By the time we got into the elevator, I was regretting my decision. Perhaps I was regretting my decision to come to Honey Massage at all. I just didn't come to Thailand for this kind of inhuman strictly business sexual encounter. I tried to put those thoughts out of my mind and focus on the beauty I was about to rub my body up against.

At least Number 42 was truly a stunner. She had a wide tall figure with an ass and tits that bulged out but not any noticeable bulges anywhere else. As she walked, her hips bounced back and forth like a runway model. I wondered if she was doing that on purpose, if she had learned to do it, or if it simply came naturally to her.

"So, are you the answer to THE question?" I asked her in the elevator.

Definitely more of a response to my demeanor than the question, her face brightened up with a big smile.

"What?" she asked.

"Number 42 is the perfect number. It's a British thing," I answered.

"Oh, I never hear that!" she said.

We exchanged names, but I forgot it immediately. I liked "Number 42" better anyway.

The upstairs of Honey Massage seemed like a redesigned hotel. There was a long hallway with equal sized rooms on either side. She led me to a room she claimed was a bigger room. It was laid out with a large bathtub near the door, a bed with old white linens in the middle and a couch and table near the window. Number 42 walked in and turned on the TV to a Thai station and then turned on the water to the tub.

An old Thai lady came in to offer me a drink. I ordered a Vodka and Red Bull. *And got some foul-tasting Thai Red Bull knockoff.*

After Number 42 was finished prepping the room, she came to sit by me. At first, I thought we were going to make out a bit on the couch while waiting for the tub to fill, but instead, she put her feet up on the table and rummaged through her purse, ignoring me the whole time. It's not that she seemed repulsed by me, she was simply bored. Waiting for the tub to fill was something she must have done hundreds of times and she thought it was a good opportunity to do chores.

The chores were checking her lottery slips. She had dozens and the task was tedious to punch them all in on her phone. Thailand is known for having no casinos, so they all must play lotteries, which arguably provide worse odds, less entertainment, and less economic stimulus. I wondered how much of her trick money she sunk into the lottery hoping to get a free ride out of her job.

"So, can you turn down a customer if you don't like the look of him?" I asked.

"No, cannot," she said.

"What happens if you do?" I asked.

"Cannot. No job," she replied.

"You get fired?"

"Yes."

I'd wondered about that sitting downstairs. It's common to hear of girls in go-go bars and other venues turning down customers for a variety of reasons. I'd even been turned down myself a few times, usually with the excuse of being on their period. The Soapies are different though, in Bangkok Soapies, for example, the girls don't even see the customer before being picked.

"How often do you not want to be picked?" I asked.

"Only Indians," she answered.

"Indians? What's wrong with Indians?" I asked.

I expected her to say they are assholes.

"They smell bad."

I chuckled. "Curry?"

"I don't know, they just smell."

44

"Well, it's a good thing you clean them off," I said. "I did not think smell would be an issue at a Soapy."

"Does not work... they still smell," she answered. "They usually don't pick me, they don't like skinny girl."

"That's good, so do the other girls like Indians? The ones that they pick more often?"

"No girl like Indians," she said.

I felt a little bad for my Indian counterparts. If the Honey Massage Soapy girls were prejudiced to them, I wondered how hard it would be for them to hook up a girl at a go-go bar.

The small talk persisted for 20 minutes or so, which was the length of time it took to fill up the bathtub. I guess they didn't feel the need to invest in better plumbing even though every bathtub in the place was to be filled and drained multiple times per day. There went a good chunk of my 90 minutes with her, most of it spent sitting apart on the couch talking about lotteries.

"Ok, are you ready?" she asked me after checking the water. It was a perfect temperature and she didn't even need to adjust it while it filled. She had some experience filling that tub.

We removed our clothes together and I finally got to see the body of Number 42. At least I managed to pick a real looker, even though she was about as exciting as a mannequin. She seemed to be around 25 with a mature body that had filled out the hips and breasts nicely. Her whole body was as white as Asian skin can get and her stomach was perfectly flat with not a trace of fat or muscles. Her long black hair was now pulled into a ponytail.

She motioned for me to get in the bathtub which I obliged eagerly, at which point she gathered her soapy kit, consisting of body wash and loofah. I momentarily scoffed at the loofah, knowing they are bacteria havens and doubting Honey Massage cared all that much about changing them out. Ah well, fuck it, if I really cared about germs, perhaps I should pick a different hobby.

She placed her kit on the edge of the bathtub and stepped gingerly between my legs. I finally felt some tingles in my crotch as the beauty knelt down and my balls rubbed against her knees as her arms draped over my encircling legs. I relaxed and let her do her thing.

First, she washed my chest, shoulders, and arms with the loofah as I made sure it didn't contact my face. Afterwards, she did the most exciting thing in the session, it was all downhill from there. I can't really explain why I felt that way, but this was the climax, maybe because it was such a big tease.

"Ok, honey, lift up," she said as she pushed up on my ass from the bottom of the tub.

I lifted my now hardening dick out of the water which placed it just below her mouth. As she used the loofah to soap down my crotch, I waited for something, anything sexual, but all I got was more mechanical washing. I don't know, honey, pretend to kiss or something! Something! But all I got was a stone-faced beautiful girl washing my crotch as if she was a nurse. By the time she slid me back under the water, I was growing limp.

After we exited the bathtub, she toweled me off and then motioned for me to lay face down on an air mattress next to the bathtub. Then she dried herself and applied oil to the front of her body.

Her body felt great rubbing on my back and butt, it was that hard Asian body with soft perky natural breasts. She caressed me in long slow circles while holding most of her weight on her arms and legs. After she flipped me, she continued the same process spending a bit of extra time rubbing her tits around my crotch and semi-hard dick. The whole time I was looking into her eyes hoping for any sort of engagement. She gave me none, though, and I eventually gave up and tried to find excitement in watching her body. Although, just a beautiful body doesn't always do it for me.

After 5 minutes, she stood up and motioned to the bed and I found myself icky in oil. I could only think perhaps the body-to-body should have happened before the bathtub, but she was probably used to doing it that way due to all the Indians and their curry! Which didn't matter anyway...

In repositioning to the bed, I noticed she grabbed a condom and held it in her hand. As I lay on my back, she began sucking my nipples with a fast tongue-flick. It was not exciting, in fact, it was annoying.

"No, no, girl, here, kiss my neck and ear," I said to her.

She was professional in that regard and moved her body up to suck and tongue-flick my ear. While doing that, she twirled her hips into my dick which started showing a little readiness. Once she felt my full erection, she lowered her body slowly while kissing my chest until she reached my dick.

In a quick motion, she slid the condom over the tip of my dick and with her mouth lengthened it down the shaft.

"Woh woh, blowjob with a condom?" I asked.

In all the time I've visited Asian sex destinations, I rarely have the girls put a condom on for the blowjob. In places like Tijuana, it's more common, but in Thailand, I was shocked. That was no fun at all.

"Yes, we are safe here," she said momentarily lifting up.

I let her blow me through the condom for half a minute or so and had enough and pulled her head up towards me. She obliged by sitting her body over my dick and pointing it in. She had a beautiful shaved pussy with moderately sized lips. I slid in gently and found it considerably tight – ode to her slim body.

I ran my hands over her soft skin to find her ass to help her grind on me. By now, she was finally looking into my eyes instead of peering off into the room, but it was too late. I was ready to get my nut and go home.

I flipped her over and pounded her pussy with all the energy I could muster. It didn't seem to faze her, she laid there taking it like a champ. Maybe she was used to much bigger than I had to offer anyway. By the time I cummed, I was dripping wet.

I pulled out and sat on my knees while she dutifully jumped up to grab some tissue and pull my condom off. That's service for you.

"Ok, you want clean?" she asked.

I did. So, we stepped into the bathtub again which had started draining but in all the time was only half drained. Not sure if that says more about the bathtub or my performance. She showered us both off and we got dressed not exchanging many words. We rode the elevator down together and as I walked out the customer exit doors, she returned to her spot on the expensive side of the lobby ready to do it again.

So far, Pattaya wasn't really doing it for me.

My third sexual encounter of the trip was far more interesting though a bit unsettling. I've never been attracted to ladyboys, but since going on sex vacations, I've told myself that I shouldn't indiscriminately avoid all contact with them. If I met one somewhere and felt an attraction to or a connection with her, I should take the physical contact as far as I could stand. Besides, it's likely the revulsion is a product of society instead of any sort of ingrained taste, and as I've matured and advanced my own sexual desires, I've grown more tolerant of the range of sexual desires that exist in the world. If I had sex with a ladyboy, I wouldn't feel judged by society. In fact, I may feel that anyone who judged me was not worth knowing. However, there is still the ick factor, and for whatever reason, it exists in me, it isn't something I can will away, which is too bad as I've heard that ladyboys give the best service.

Tinder in Pattaya is simply a means of hooking up with freelancers, and there are lots of ladyboys, most of which are clearly identified. After all, it would do them no good to show up at a customer's request and deal with an irate man upset that he wasn't getting a pussy to fuck. "Top and Bottom" is a phrase I was introduced to which means they give as well as they get.

I spent hours in my first two days while jet lagged browsing through the selection on Tinder and weeding out all the ladyboys. Of the girls that were left, most of them were very clear on their profiles they were freelancers only having links to other social media and a statement that said: "100% lady, don't ask me!" Mary's profile was one of those that said 100% lady, but along with that contained an actual profile that talked like a girl looking for a husband. "Looking tall and handsome" "want man to take care of me" were some of the phrases on her profile. Her pictures, well, they were beautiful. If her pictures had been on a profile in America, she'd have her selection of wealthy, handsome men.

When we matched and she began having a real conversation with me, instead of straight to "wanna fuck?" I suspected something was rotten in the state of Chon Buri, but while my sex tourist instincts were sounding alerts, there were some signs that she might be just a regular girl turning tricks on the side while looking for a man. First, her English was near perfect, and that seemed to back up her claim that she had come to Pattaya to be a teacher from the Philippines.

I worked out a strategy for when I chose to meet her. My first consideration was if she turned up and looked nothing like her pics. That would be easy, I'd just tell her to meet me in the lobby so I could turn her away without knowing which condo I was in. The second consideration was if she was a ladyboy. If she was, she'd certainly be a post-op, and figure she could pass for a lady completely. She probably couldn't, but I figured if she looked like her pics, it would be worth the experience.

I was on the treadmill around 8 am in the morning when she messaged me asking if I wanted to fuck her. At least now she was sounding more like a freelancer, and she caught me at the perfect time. After getting a price of 1,500 baht, I told her to come straight over and I finished my workout while waiting. When she messaged again she was pulling up to the condo, I ran down the stairs to the lobby just in time to see her walking up. There was no doubt it was the girl from the pictures. She looked ravishing. She looked so good, my instincts went on high alert again. The other shoe was bound to drop at some point.

She had slightly tanned fair Asian skin and wasn't wearing any makeup. There were no pimples anywhere that I could see. She was wearing short white jean shorts showing off the same skinny gorgeous legs from her profile, and a green tank top exposing thin lady-like arms. Her boobs were certainly bigger than the average Asian, but I could not tell at that point if they were silicone. She had long flowing highlighted hair and smiled a half-breed smile with big full lips that looked European.

When she spoke, she sounded like a lady, but I did pick up the slightest ladyboy twang. I began to figure that she was a post-op like I had suspected, but I still wasn't 100% sure. Besides, I wanted to go through with it either way, so long as a dick didn't pop out. I was 100% sure THAT wasn't going to happen.

"Hi Nathan, it's nice to meet you, I'm Mary," she said as I showed her to the elevator. Her English was fluent, she may even have been able to speak it better than me and she had the distinctive educated Filipino accent I'd heard many times. Besides being a higher-level conversation, and even though I was looking intently for an Adam's Apple, the interaction seemed like any of the other interactions I've had with sex workers. She was comfortable, I was comfortable, nothing but two people about to go screw.

Never, ever, leave a freelancer alone in your room.

When we arrived at the condo, I offered her a drink and jumped in the shower. This is not something I'd recommend with a freelancer, but I had most everything locked up in the safe and anything else of value she could grab was in my closet which I could still see from the shower. While in the shower, I heard her go through a plastic bag from the Nike store that was still sitting on the floor by the door. I guess she thought something new might still be in it, she'd be wrong, it was just my trash bag. In any event, I took my shower in a flash before she got any better ideas.

We chatted for a while about her time as a teacher in Thailand and where she was from in the Philippines. I was making a bit of a connection with her, that only deepened when she said, "I never thought I'd become a hooker." She didn't seem new to the business, but like many other girls found it an easy way to make a living while in between gigs.

"Can I have my money?" she asked.

I had nearly forgotten my previous worries when she asked this question, but they came rushing back. When asked for the money up front, I'm always worried there will be some reason I may not want to pay afterward, but since the price was only 1,500 baht which I probably would pay just not wanting to cause a scene, I ponied it up.

"Ok, are you ready?" she asked. *Yes, yes, I'm always ready!*

At this point, I was still not convinced she was a ladyboy. There were a few inconclusive hints, but when she took off her top, leaving her shorts on and crawled into bed, and I was exposed to a perfect set of silicone implants, I became convinced... I was about to have a sexual encounter with a post-op ladyboy that I had already paid. Oh well, I might as well dive in. I sucked on those tits while she pushed my head in for several minutes and as I pulled her nipples as deep in my throat as I could, she began to moan an indisputable ladyboy whine.

"Honey, do you have condom?" she asked.

I jumped up to open the closet while she got up and headed for her purse and took her shorts off. Of course, I wanted to see the shorts come off. In the back of my mind, I was still a little afraid a dick would pop out, though if it did, she'd be the most feminine ladyboy I'd ever seen.

I never saw a dick, but things got real when I saw her butt. It was not a feminine butt, it was an Asian man ass, just like all the ones I'd seen in Asian porn. This view was the first glimpse I saw of the mutant she was. A perfect lady upper body, a perfect set of legs, a perfect face, and then there was this disgusting Asian dude ass. Somebody should have told her to do squats. I began to get a little nervous and wasn't sure I'd be able to go through with it, but the sight didn't last long. She knew to hide her backside. She turned around quickly and applied lubricant to a big, but normal looking vagina, at least as normal as I could make out in the dim light.

The blowjob was great, just as it should be from a ladyboy. It was my first, but I'd heard about them from many other sex tourists. Ladyboys give the best blowjobs and I'd have to agree with it, and that's even despite that she did it with a condom on. "I'm a safety girl," she said, and never backed off even in the face my strong objections. If I had it to do over again, I would have told her to finish with the blowjob, but I suppose then I wouldn't have had this experience to tell.

When she climbed on top, I got a better look at her vagina. It was huge! There was a long slit running from deep between her legs all the way to the front. There was no clit, it was all lips and I couldn't even make out a hole where she was going to put my dick. At the front of the vagina, I could make out a scar, obviously where her previous plumbing had been removed. I couldn't help but point it out and lean in closer for a better a look.

"Oh yea, I had an ovarian cyst when I was younger," she said—a statement she had prepared.

All I could do was laugh, I didn't even realize she still believed I thought she was a woman – or born a woman to be more precise. In respect to her, everything about her except a man-butt and a strangely shaped pussy was very feminine, and to a total naïve man, she might have actually passed off the ovarian surgery explanation.

"Sure. Just bear with me, this is my first time," I said.

"What? Do you think I'm a ladyboy?' she asked.

"It's ok, I'm ok with it," I said.

"I'm not ladyboy! I'm lady!" she said.

It should have been me who was insulted. I'd decided before she even came that should this scenario play out, I was going to go on with it, but I would have much preferred to be able to discuss it. I had questions I wanted to ask. However, with the nervousness that already existed and being completely new to the situation gave me pause and instead I just said, "Ok, let's flip."

Seeing her body stretch out on the bed helped with my feelings of manhood. I thought she was a truly beautiful creature I was about to fuck, what does it matter if she used to be a man? I mounted myself on my arms and positioned my dick to enter her as she grabbed it and helped to coerce it in. It was tight! By God, it was tight. It didn't even feel like a hole that was possible to enter. I definitely wasn't trying to enter an ass, her legs were almost flat on the bed, this crafted pussy had the strength of a vice grip.

"I didn't have sex all day yesterday, you are my first customer for two days," she said.

I smiled at yet another lame excuse. Sorry girl, real pussies just don't work like that.

"Ok, push," she said after half a minute of trying to work my dick inside. That's what I did, I pushed. I put all my weight on my erect penis and it didn't go anywhere.

"Ouch, wait wait wait."

I was becoming amused at the situation and the thought hit me that if she was a real girl, I'd have hit the jackpot.

She repositioned my dick a little more and commanded that I push again. This time, my dick found the target and my entire shaft slid inside between two walls of solid cartilage.

"Oh, that's the way, honey, fuck me!"

I had indeed found "the way," and I proceeded to pound that manufactured pussy as hard as I could. I didn't feel any need to hold back. At that point, the genuine ladyboy wail made another appearance, and I realized I was fucking my first transsexual – or lady that was once a man – or just fuck it, who cares about labels? I looked at the lady below me... beautiful. Then, I leaned in to suck on her tongue.

"Oh no, honey, I don't kiss on the mouth," she said.

Well, this girl was acting as much like a stuck-up female hooker as I'd ever been with. Oh well, I just got back to plowing her. Though I was very turned on by the idea of adding to my sex inventory, between being lied to and now denied so simple a thing as a kiss on the lips, I was ready to bust my nut and be done with it.

As I thrust deeper into her, I tried various tactics to see if I could cause her any type of discomfort. I'd very my angle a bit, pull out slowly and then pound back in as hard as I could, but nothing seemed to bring out any kind of pain in her. In fact, her pussy was loosening up. The vice grip that felt like two bones squeezing my dick at first now felt more like two filled balloons. One thing is for sure, this self-expanding pussy could never pass for the real thing. I wondered if the doctor that did her was one of the best or if she merely looked for the best deal.

After I finished and pulled out, she bounded up towards the bathroom giving me another peek at the Asian man butt. That was truly a hideous sight, she got everything right except that.

"Oh, I love fucking!" she said.

"How long have you been a freelancer?" I asked.

"Two months, since I broke up with my boyfriend," she replied.

I got the story she met a Japanese man while teaching, that took her on vacations in Thailand and spoiled her to death. I guess she got used to the good lifestyle and decided to take up hooking. I believed her that she came to Thailand to teach. She was obviously well-educated.

"I think you should tell your customers the truth, you will get yourself into trouble someday," I said.

"What do you mean?" she asked.

"Never mind," I answered.

I wondered if she was in denial about it. Did she want to forget that she was ever a man, or did she simply feel it would be less profitable to admit to being a post-op? I'm sure it is way less profitable to be a post-op ladyboy. She really isn't a girl, but definitely not a man either. Many men have an attraction to ladyboys with dicks. I don't fully understand that desire... but those men don't go for post-ops, and men who like girls would just rather find a girl that had always been a girl. You can find some sympathy for post-op's, like a person born of parents from two different races, who are limited to choosing partners from tolerant individuals. A post-op will be attracted to heterosexual men but will be limited to those men who will be attracted to her despite her post-op status, and never because of it.

After she got dressed, I asked her to turn around so I could lift her shirt and check out her ass in her shorts. It looked like a sexy girl's ass, just like some girls who wear clothes well but look terrible when their fat flops out.

"Wait, I will walk you to the elevator," I said to her as I looked around for my headphones. I was planning to finish the workout that I interrupted to meet her. Looking back, there was an awkwardness in her demeanor as I fumbled about the condo searching for where I had laid them down.

At the time, I only thought her as impatient and told her she could go. It took a couple of minutes for me to realize the most likely location of my headphones: in her purse. I assume since she couldn't find anything of value to steal, she simply grabbed whatever was laying around. I had not included them among items that needed to be locked up while I was in the shower. I ran out of the condo and towards the elevator, with all the speed I could muster, but by the time I got to the lobby and outside the building, she was gone. She must have had a driver waiting for her, as there was no way she could have ran out through security without being stopped to ask what all the rush was about.

The security of the condo will stop lone Thai girls but tends to let vehicles in and out without much fuss.

So, my first ladyboy pay-for-sex experience went down in the manner they are often described: liars, cheats, and thieves. Despite having the experience mostly under control, I spent the rest of the day in a state of depression. I felt like I was scammed with being lied to about her ladyboy status, and even though I knew the truth from the start, I don't enjoy being played. By itself, that may not have affected me, but when my headphones were stolen, it made me feel like a total mark, and though being a sex tourist means I must put up with being marked occasionally, it isn't very common anymore for me to feel actually taken advantage of.

The headphones weren't expensive, but they fit me well when walking, and even in the States, I have trouble finding ones that fit. I replaced them with a pair that didn't really fit at all.

Never, ever, leave a freelancer alone in your room.

3

What a difference a girl makes

Besides a shopping trip to replace my headphones, I spent the next morning after my ladyboy encounter isolating and second-guessing my decisions. What could have been an interesting first sexual experience instead was something I wanted to forget. By late afternoon, I was worked up and needed a beer desperately.

In every direction from my condo was a Beer Bar. Beer Bars or Beer Gardens give Thailand character. I've never traveled anywhere that has bars quite like them. In some areas of Pattaya, there are mile-long streets filled with nothing but Beer Bars.

What identifies them as Beer Bars are the long, usually rectangle bars dotted throughout a large roofed area but lacking walls or entranceways. Around the bars are stools where customers and girls sit and mingle. Some bars will have other lounge style chairs and pool tables and some will be strictly the bar. Some of the bars employ girls who dance on a small stage in the middle of the bars for all to see, from the inebriated bar patrons to the passersby outside. Almost all of them have girls who sit with customers and sell drinks. Most, but not all, of the girls who work in beer bars will leave with the customer on a barfine.

I left my condo and crossed Second Road heading for the first open Beer Bar. It was still early in the afternoon so I ended up walking a way down Second Road and down Soi 7 until I finally found one that looked open, though actually, there were a few open but it would have been me heads-up with an unattractive bartender. I was looking more for a place I could sit, have a beer, and be invisible, but with some eye candy – female eye candy. I was in the mood to purge the tranny fever from my body.

I never saw the name of the bar, and later in my trip, I never could find the bar again. The turnover in bar employees and clientele can cause one bar to entirely change its appearance from one night to the next. Or maybe it was simply that I never found the person I was looking for.

He appeared as a generic Pattaya tourist – a 60-year-old bald white man with what hair he had being jet black, a cratered face and oversized nose and oversized glasses, with a pudgy body to go with his oversized mug of beer. I didn't remember his name, but I'll call him Frank, it seems to fit.

"You look like a man on a mission," he said to me in a voice so deep it would not have surprised me if his job was in voice acting or radio host, the only characteristic about him that stood out.

He was referring to my nearly empty mug of beer that had been served to me barely 2 minutes previously.

My first reaction to Frank was one of annoyance, and I only nodded my head without turning towards him.

"How long have you been in Pattaya?" he continued.

There was something soothing about his voice and adding to that his unassuming attitude and friendliness, I lightened up to him.

"Less than a week, what about you?" I responded while motioning to the bartender for another beer.

"Oh..." he said slowly and calmly in that deep relaxed voice, "I've been here a while."

"You live here?" I asked.

"Yea... almost 10 years now. Well... not in Pattaya. I have some... medical problems that I'm here for. I spent most of the time in Northern Isaan[5]," he said.

"You lived in Isaan?" I asked. "Were you working there?"

"Oh... no." Frank spoke in a slow deliberate way that with his deep voice impressed upon the listener that whatever he had to say was deeply meaningful. It wasn't, but at the time I was hooked to his every word, which could have also been the state I was in. Perhaps I was impressionable at the time.

"I managed to sell everything I owned at the height of the bubble in 2005. I couldn't live in Pattaya on that money, but I could in Isaan...

"Well, I thought I could. It's all gone now," he sighed.

"So, what do you do for money now?" I asked

"Generous friends," he said with a hint of a pained look. "I'm on my way home after I get some more tests on my heart done."

"So, Thailand cost more than you thought?" I asked.

I had a general idea of the costs of living in Thailand and other countries in Southeast Asia. I would consider $2000 per month minimum as moving there while sacrificing a western salary seemed to defeat the purpose. I enjoy my frequent trips, but it seems to me that living in Thailand with the salary of a Thai would take the fun out of

---

[5] Isaan – Refers to Northeast Thailand. Draw a line straight north from Bangkok. Everything east of the line and north of Cambodia is Isaan. 90% of the sex workers come from there.

it. Everything becomes monotonous when you do it every day, and when you couldn't buy pussy at least every weekend, holy God, why would you want to live there?

"Oh… I could have easily never worked again. …. That …. Was the plan," he said chuckling.

"It's… the sex… the sex … got me."

Moving to Southeast Asia with plenty of money and then overspending on sex and women is a story I've heard many times. Most guys believe they can get a girlfriend and she'll continue to live like a local, eating rice and dried fish, but instead, she insists on certain luxuries that tend to have similar costs to having a girlfriend in a western country. Or, they simply won't be able to have relationships with the simple women and instead slowly bleed themselves on sex workers and gold diggers. Frank was the later.

The utterly unattractive bartender made an appearance about this time and spoke to Frank in Thai. Frank turned away from me and brightened up as if she was the love of his life and answered her in Thai. As she retrieved another beer for him, I discovered Frank was quite the charming man. In that short exchange, he had her beaming with joy.

"How long did it take to learn Thai?" I asked him.

"Oh… I'm still not fluent. It took… 2 years… to even be comfortable where I lived. Five years before I could date a girl that didn't speak English," he answered.

The waitress returned with another beer for me which I promptly began downing.

Don't pick up a ladyboy on the street. Duh.

"So… tell me… what's got you pounding those beers?" he asked.

"Had my first ladyboy," I answered.

Frank chuckled softly, though my answer didn't faze him. Then I told the whole story about meeting Mary on Tinder and getting my earphones stolen.

"Oh man," Frank said. "She's not even a ladyboy."

"Post-op ladyboy," I argued.

Frank sighed. "Son, those aren't ladyboys. … Ladyboys… have dicks. You ain't been with a ladyboy … until you have a lady shove her dick in your ass.

"Or… maybe… when you fuck a ladyboy in the ass… with one hand on her balls and the other on a tit.

"Or… Sixty-nine her…"

Shit got real with Mr. Average-Joe Frank really fucking fast. I wondered if his dick was getting hard as he described the acts that qualify as sex with a tranny. Guys who are open about their sexual inventory are rarer than you'd think at a sex destination.

"So, how many ladyboys have you been with?" I asked.

"pfft… … hundreds," he answered.

"You like ladyboys more than girls?" I asked.

"Oh… no… I just like sex. And… Thai ladyboys really love sex," he answered.

"So, what happened your first time? Was it like mine?" I asked.

"Nothing at all like yours. I wish…" he said.

"Mine was…" he continued. "Nana Plaza over 20 years ago. I was new to Thailand then, it was my first trip alone. I was… well… let's just say my life at home was in shambles. I was a mess… and… I guess she picked up on it. Cause… though I blacked out most of it… I woke up with a sore ass…

63

dried cum everywhere… I do mean fucking everywhere… and no wallet or passport… thank God she left my clothes."

I wasn't sure whether to laugh or cry. I was certainly amazed he opened up so easily. It did a lot to belittle my encounter with a post-op. I listened to Frank detail more of the story, of a middle-aged man looking to get lost in Thailand, happening on an aggressive ladyboy on the street, and because of the depth of his depression, lost any sense of inhibition. There is a good rule here: Don't pick up a ladyboy on the street. Duh.

The details of Frank's story are for another time…

"So, you liked it so much you decided to fuck hundreds more?" I asked him.

He slapped me on the shoulder and laughed.

"I guess afterward… it just wasn't a big deal anymore. You should try it… you never know… you might just get your world rocked. Most… will do anything… crazy as fuck… Fuck their face until they vomit… Piss on them… And they'll put anything up your ass… anything. I prefer their tongues, myself," he answered.

"Not even close to my experience, Frank," I said.

"Because yours… wasn't a ladyboy… as I told you."

Is that what it would come to for me? I'd pushed all kinds of boundaries on my sex trips, I didn't even think there was much else I could do with girls… there was no Porn Star experience I had not yet done, but I'd never been with a ladyboy, at least not a true ladyboy as Frank would describe. I'd sure had my chances, and though I told myself I wouldn't be opposed to it if I became attracted to one, that attraction would have to be extreme as the thought of playing around with a dick was repulsive. I'd gag before I had the chance to be gagged.

As the sun began to set and the crowds appeared, I had had my fill of talking about dicks with Frank. It seemed I had wasted an entire day without even a thought of pussy. Pussy was the reason I was in Pattaya! I was tired, but I needed to fuck a pussy. I needed to wipe away the tranny fever. I decided to get a real massage and then head back to Honey Massage. That would be quick and easy and I could probably be in bed within three hours. There was just one problem.

"Hey Frank, do you know a good legitimate massage? No happy endings," I asked.

"Legitimate? Oh, if you want a real massage, any of the ones with uniforms are good," he answered.

I looked at him blankly and almost busted up laughing. I may have been a Thailand newbie, but I knew damn well most of those would still want to jerk you off for a tip. Maybe "legitimate" has a different meaning to a Thailand regular.

I said my goodbyes to Frank and staggered out of the Beer Bar.

Even though I trusted my own instincts on the subject of massages, I decided to test that idea since I had no better idea of my own. Uniformed massage parlors in Pattaya are all legitimate? Ok...

There was a collection of massage parlors in a shopping center between my condo and the Avenue Pattaya[6]. There were always decent looking women[7] out front hawking

---

[6] A collection of restaurants, including Starbucks, on Second Road just north of Soi 13.

massages and being on Second Road instead of Soi Honey or Soi Buakhao, I figured they stood a decent chance of being real massage parlors.

As I approached, I slowed to a stroll as the girls placed on point began to call at me. "Hey, handsome, you want massage?"

They were wearing the standard massage uniform in Thailand, which I find sexy as hell. It's a tight shirt, usually white, and a long tight skirt with a simple design. The girls in front are usually the most attractive though there are always girls sitting around who should be working in a kitchen practically spilling out of the tight uniform.

I made a lap around the massage parlors until I saw a girl that I fancied. She was probably around 30, skinny with long black hair. She smiled at me excitedly when I made eye contact and she jumped up and grabbed my arm to take me inside. "Where are you from?" she asked.

"America, how do you know I want massage?" I asked her as I let her drag me inside.

"I can just tell, you are hungry for me. You need me rub you," she said.

She certainly didn't talk like a legitimate masseuse. For sure she'd go for my dick at the end of the massage, but maybe I'd just let her stroke it for a while. That is a strategy I use as it can help with the encounter later.

---

[7] Uniformed massage parlors often have girls still eager to perform sexual services. To clearly show your intentions for massage only, insist on a massage in the public room, and don't pick a pretty girl. Though some have management that won't allow it. These are often close to more touristy areas and generally are nicer. Chivarame massage just north of Central Mall on Second Road is an example of one where handjobs are prohibited. For up to date info, see web site.

We passed the ugly girls sitting in front of the large glass pane as we walked inside. The sight when I stepped inside is something I never want to see again. On either side were long benches set up for foot massages. There were four on each side and all but one was filled with Indians. They all had just received a foot massage and were just lying there with their big feet sticking out the end of the bench. It's as if we were walking through an armed guard of feet! Jesus Christ guys, just veg out... and I swear some were holding their crotch, must have been some great foot massages.

We stepped gingerly through the Lotrimin patch and arrived at a back desk with a sign for prices of massages.

"Oil massage," she said to the older Thai lady behind the desk.

"Uhh... how about Thai massage?" I asked.

I like Thai massages. First, I'm not a big fan of oil even before my Honey Massage experience, but I like the stretching and other voodoo they do on the body. I get oil massages everywhere, and at this particular massage parlor, the oil massage was 450 baht and the Thai massage was 300 baht. No way did I want an oil massage.

"Oh ok," said my masseuse. "Most farang[8] want oil massage."

After paying the 300 baht, she led me up a narrow staircase. It gave me a great view of her body. She was a skinny thing, with just a slight definition of an ass poking through the tight black flowered skirt as she walked gingerly up the stairs. It was enough to attract me more to her, I wondered if she'd mind if I grabbed that ass. I thought

---

[8] Farang – White foreigner, in case you didn't know!

67

better of it though, there was still a small chance this was a legitimate massage. You certainly couldn't get away with that at a massage parlor in the states.

There was a large room with over 20 foam mattresses laid out against the walls with 3 ongoing massages on the first three as we walked in. I immediately thought there was no way she was going to put me on the 4th one. This huge room and they use the first 3 spots? What is the deal with that?

She didn't attempt to put me on the 4th mattress though, she led me to a side room with 3 mattresses and a door. The door was open at the bottom for about a foot but otherwise granted total separation from the rest of the parlor. Well, this wasn't going to be a legitimate massage, that's for sure. Was it something about my white skin or did I just exude pervert?

"Ok, here for Thai massage," she said and handed me a grey drab one-piece outfit to wear. Then she disappeared out the door and pulled it to.

I removed my clothes and then pondered the little outfit. It was way too big for me. I'm not a big guy, but I can't imagine they get many customers that needed XXXL. There was one large tie that attached to the back... at least I thought it was the back, but there didn't seem to be any definition on either side. I decided to just throw it over my shoulders and let her fix it when she came back.

As I waited, I wondered what might go on in that private room. She would certainly offer extra services, but would it be full service? Maybe I could knock out a decent massage and get laid in one stop.

It wasn't but a minute when she knocked on the door, "Hello, ready?"

When she opened, I was standing and she looked at me and chuckled at the outfit hanging off my shoulders.

"Wait, I fix," she said.

She pulled the drab up and I ducked my head to let it slip off exposing my naked body to her. Well, we could have avoided a couple of steps, I thought.

"Oh, sexy man, haha," she laughed.

She twirled the outfit around to find the holes then slipped my arm through a hole and worked her way around my body to the other arm caressing my butt and when she moved around to tie the cord in front, she made no effort to keep from slapping my dick and balls which dangled inside the outfit. It was oddly arousing.

Once she finished tying, she dropped her hand straight down and rubbed across my dick and smiled. She was a good girl, this massage might be fun.

"Ok, lay down here," she said, pointing to the middle mattress.

I dropped to the mattress face down and she sat on her knees beside me and began a half-decent though very short Thai massage. A Thai massage is different from massages in western countries. It is mostly pressure and stretching. A good masseuse can really limber up a body. Even though I was probably twice the size of her, she did a good job of gaining leverage to pull on my joints.

The outfit limited her ability to tease me, but at many points in the massage, she would rub her hands over my ass and up between my legs to fondle my balls. The massage itself was good, but she kept me aroused through most of it.

After only twenty minutes, I was on my back and she was kneeling over my feet. Unexpectedly, she reached her hand up to my crotch and grabbed my dick.

"You want massage here?" she asked with a big smile.

Well, that probably settled the question of whether I could get laid in this little room. If there were options, she wouldn't have asked specifically about a handjob. So, I settled into my original plan of getting stroked for a bit, but not cumming.

"Oh, of course," I said.

I would have preferred a longer massage. So much for all uniformed massage parlors being legitimate.

She repositioned herself between my legs and untied the robe letting it fall to the sides, how convenient. She stood there over my hardening dick slowly caressing and smiling at me as if a young girl teasing me.

Then she bent her head down as if to give me a blowjob but stopped short of actually inserting it in her mouth. What the fuck? I dropped my head back in disappointment and she laughed.

"One second honey," she said and leaped up to grab oil.

When she returned, she dropped her little ass down right under my shoulder and faced toward my dick. This position seemed to give her good leverage and it allowed me to play with her ass. She had a sexy skinny body from behind for sure, a tiny waist but with a little meat on her ass giving a slight voluptuous look.

"Boom boom?" I asked her in desperation.

"No, sorry, no boom boom here," she answered stoically. *I knew the answer before I asked it.*

I relaxed and watched her stroking me. She started off slow but within a minute or so had increased her pace furiously with both hands. She was a master at handjobs and very strong as well. Her technique was perfect for me, using both hands to slide from base to head while keeping as much of my shaft in her grasp the whole time. Her elbows were pointed to the sides and she was leaned over so her face was less than a foot above the head of my dick.

Her little tease blowjob had stuck in my mind, and I kept hoping she would drop her head down and engulf me in her mouth. With every head bob down, I got more hopeful and with every bob up, I became disheartened.

Once I gave up obsessing about getting a blowjob, my mind wandered back to the events of the last 24 hours. I thought, "Is she a ladyboy? Is that why there is no boom boom?"

It was virtually impossible this masseuse was a ladyboy, but my brain at that point was fucked up. As she continued stroking vigorously, I began to reason myself into the conclusion she was a ladyboy. From that view, it was possible. She had long straight hair that was covering her face. The most visible part of her body was her arms which were slightly muscular from the years of working as a masseuse.

Was my entire trip destined to be nothing but ladyboys?

I began to lose all interest in shopping around for sex and resigned myself to cumming via a handjob from a ladyboy. I relaxed, stared at the ceiling, and let it flow.

"Oh, good job honey. Very strong," she said.

She jumped up to grab some tissue and her very feminine body and face came into view and I giggled at myself for the insane thoughts. 100% lady.

She was smiling like she loved her job as she cleaned the cum from my dick and her hands. She missed most of it though which had dripped down to my hips and belly.

"You want more massage?" she asked.

Well, of course, I did.

There was no hot towel or any extra effort to clean up the cum. She rearranged the outfit back over me and the cum spread out inside it. I could feel several drops of cum in the robe. I wondered how many other drops of dried cum were in contact with me besides my own.

Despite my attention to all the cum dispersed over my body as she continued the Thai massage, I enjoyed the rest of the hour, now that my concerns about her ladyboy status were alleviated.

"Ok, all done," she said finally, patted me on the butt and left the room, pulling the door behind her.

I laid in that dingy massage room with little dots of cum all over my body processing the events of the day and the trip so far. Besides an extremely entertaining conversation with an expat, things were not really working out how I had hoped. Surely, it couldn't get any worse, right?

After getting dressed, I realized no mention of a tip was made at all. I guess she expected me to know the going rate? Or maybe she suspected I was new to town and could ask a higher price. Usually, I consider it in my favor when the girl does not mention her price beforehand, but I wasn't in the mood to stand fast against getting high balled.

I had a 500 baht note, and I decided to hand it to her as I stepped out of the room.

"Thank you, honey," she said while placing her hands together in front of her chin in a prayer manner. I wondered if even 500 baht[9] was too much. Oh well, getting jerked off

---

[9] As of the publication of this book (2019), most masseuses in Pattaya are asking for 1000 baht for handjob and 1500 for blowjob

in a massage parlor back home would run at least 2000 baht.

My day was now over. There would be no sex, I was exhausted and made my way back to the condo. I vowed that the next day I'd hit some go-go bars and find some real satisfaction, and forget about the ladyboy phobia I had built up in my head.

4

A mess from the elevator

3 AM. Jet lag can be excruciating in the early stages of a trip to Asia. I woke up after only four hours of sleep to that groggy slow-processing feeling of insomnia. In that state, my instincts and desires took more control over my thoughts and my libido goes into overdrive. As I laid there in bed rearranging my hard-on for comfort, I retraced the events of the last few days and how they could have been better. Outside, I could hear the calls of a ladyboy's high-pitched voice. She was probably on Soi Honey yelling at a foreigner on his way home.

It seemed I was being inundated with ladyboys. I couldn't even escape them at 3 AM lying alone in my condo. I desperately wanted to pound some 18-year-old girl to reaffirm my manhood, but where would I find one at 3 AM? Surely, there had to be some late-night bars with freelancers somewhere, but I didn't have a clue where to look, except for Beach Road.

I dragged myself out of bed, and fixed some coffee, trying to wipe the exhaustion from my face. I still felt as if it was the first day of the trip, as none of my sexual encounters had been satisfying.

There was only one thing to do… head out into the city of Pattaya and find a girl to cheer me up. I figured I'd walk down Soi Honey to Soi Buakhao, maybe something would be open or I'd meet a girl going home. If that didn't work out, I'd make the walk over to Beach Road, there was bound to be some desperate girl.

I left my condo and went towards the elevator. The BASE condo closes all but one elevator at night. Why they do that is beyond my comprehension. Not only does it seem unnecessary but wouldn't it cause problems for everyone if that one elevator broke down… or some couple decided to fuck around in it?

The elevator was on its way to a high floor to pick someone up. I was giddy in anticipation as the elevator made its way down to my floor.

When age is in doubt, move on.

The door opened and a young-looking girl in a tight, red, one-piece dress appeared. She had a cute face if you could look past her exhausted expression. Her body was slim with barely any humps, besides the obvious impressions made by her training bra. Her hair was in a ponytail and her eye shadow was slightly smudged. It seemed she'd had a long night.

I entered the elevator next to her and turned my head at her like a perv.

"Hello, cutie. Where do you work?" I asked.

"I'm freelancer," she said.

She turned her head to look at me, immediately understanding that I was in the market. She didn't act excited in the least bit though. In fact, I got the sense she wanted to go home but would be willing to entertain an offer.

"How old are you?" I asked.

"17," she answered.

Shit.

Well, there goes that idea.

I said, "Oh" and turned away from her waiting for the elevator door to open on the bottom floor.

The moment I turned away and acted uninterested, she came alive. Her face turned to one of aggression as if she was a girl about to engage in a cat fight. She grabbed my crotch and pulled herself into my body, looking up at me from about the height of my shoulders.

"You no want me?" she asked frowning.

"No, sorry," I said.

About this time, the elevator door opened. I began to move forward, but she stood in front pushing against me and began to stroke my crotch as she leaned in and kissed my neck.

"Wait," she said.

Look… thing is, I'm not a robot. When a cute girl goes all aggressive on me, my dick is going to react, and with all the disappointments in my vacation so far, it reacted instantly. She found it in my pants, she grabbed it with her thumb and index finger and began stroking it, as she continued munching on my neck.

When the elevator door closed, I relaxed and let her push me back against the wall. She was turning me on. I tried to fight my desire, but in the end, my lust took over, and I rolled my head and looked down at her and allowed her to stick her tongue in my mouth.

Rum… she was wasted. Again, I had a very good reason to get the hell out of the elevator and let her go her own way, but I didn't. I grabbed her ass and pulled her into me and she responded by smashing her lips harder into mine. She was kissing me not in a passionate way, but in a violent way. She bit my bottom lip and pulled away and when it slipped out from her teeth she smirked.

Then she dropped to her knees and grabbed my belt and began undoing it. Shit, was I going to get a blowjob right here in the elevator? As she undid my pants, I grabbed them to keep them up. Admittedly, I was having fun at that point. She slid her hand through the fly in my underwear and found my dick and pulled it out.

So, here I am with a barely underage girl in the single working elevator of a crowded condo building at 4 AM about to get a blowjob, with no mention yet of money.

"You want me smoke?" she asked.

Probably, the fun would have ended at that point. You see, in Thailand, the age of consent is 15[10], but that does not apply to prostitution, so the moment I agreed to sexual service for an exchange of money, I'd be committing a compoundable offense, or in other words, Thai prison. Of course, none of that shit really matters anyway. Did you know prostitution is illegal in Thailand regardless of age? The only thing that matters is what the cops want to pin on you, but that doesn't mean you should give them any easy excuses. The most important rule I have for sex tourism was about to be broken. When age is in doubt, move on. Whereas a bargirl's age is rarely in doubt, a girl being of age is never assured when picking up on the street, online, or a crazy bitch in the elevator. In my case, it wasn't even in doubt...

---

[10] This is the common perception and what I believed at the time, though in doing research for this book, I discovered instances of men being prosecuted for statutory rape when the girl was 16 and the man was over 18, even without prostitution involved.

Not a second after she asked that question, the elevator began moving up. I panicked and lunged forward to press the button for my floor as she continued holding my dick. I prayed it would not stop on a floor before mine.

She seemed oblivious, she still sat on her knees holding my dick with an angry scowl on her face, as if I was forcing her to hold my dick. Ah fuck it, I thought. If the elevator door opens on a floor other than mine, I'll deal with it then. I leaned against the side wall, and she began tugging on me still staring into my eyes menacingly.

The door opened on my floor and no one was there.

"Ok, out!" I barked at her.

She stood up and walked out of the elevator dragging me by the cock. Through all that, I was still rock hard. Once I passed into the hall, I stopped, crossed my arms and motioned to her as if to say, "hey, you going to let go of my dick or what?"

"You want smoke? I smoke you, I'm good, see…" and with that, she dropped to her knees and took me in her mouth.

Mr. Thai Police Chief sir… she never mentioned money.

I was lost to that feeling of pleasure confused by the fear of committing a serious crime, not to mention a wholly immoral act, and compounded by the knowledge someone could step out of their condo at any time. I braced myself against the wall attempting to will myself out of the desire to let this young sexy mouth finish her work. She really was good. Her tongue was pressed against the bottom of my shaft as she bobbed her head rapidly.

Where did she learn how to give such a good blowjob? At 17, how many could she possibly have given? I'm not sure I wanted to know the answer to that question, but of all the thoughts that raced through my mind, the only one I acted on was the desire not to get caught in the hallway of the condo.

"Ok, let's go to my condo," I said.

She pulled away and wiped her mouth, again with that terror scowl.

I fixed my pants on the walk to the condo and she followed close behind. Opening the door, I expected to be attacked in the same way she attacked me in the elevator, but instead, she casually walked around my condo poking through everything. It was unnerving, it seemed she was scouting for things to steal.

She looked through the cabinets by the TV stand, the bathroom, the kitchen cabinets, and even the refrigerator, as I stood there like a dummy. When she walked into the bedroom, I followed her, mostly to pay attention to what she was rifling through. I sat on the end of the bed confused.

Finally, she stood in front of me.

"You pay me," she commanded.

"I'm sorry, you're too young, I can't pay you *right now*," I responded.

I thought I was being cute and trying to work a legal loophole. I wrongly expected her to understand that I'd pay her afterward. Whether it was lost in translation or if she was just plain nuts, the conversation took a bad turn.

"No, mother fucker!" she said slightly raising her voice.

Until that point, I somehow managed to miss the signs this girl was a raving lunatic.

"I smoke already, you fucking pay!" she yelled, this time quite loud.

"Ok ok," I said trying to quiet her down. I stood up and took my money out. I had a wad on me which she noticed but I only pulled out a 500 baht note. I figured 500 baht was plenty for a forced one-minute blowjob in the elevator.

"Here, and you can go," I said as I walked toward the door.

When I reached the door, she collided with it keeping it shut and then she dropped to her knees again and reached for my crotch, but this time she didn't find a hard member. I fought to keep her hands away as she struggled with me.

"Wait, no, I smoke more," she growled.

I was keeping her from pulling on my pants, but also trying not to manhandle her. Finally, she gave up and put her hands down to her sides and then let loose the most high-pitched ear-piercing shriek I've ever heard. The entire floor probably heard it.

I instinctively grabbed her to pull her away from the door, opened it, and then shoved her out, the whole time she was fighting and yelling, "No... no... no."

Once I had her outside, I tried to close the door, but she lunged at me and managed to get an arm through.

"MOTHER FUCKER!" she yelled at the top of her lungs.

I tried for a bit to push her out, but finally, I decided it would be best to go outside and escort her down to the elevator. As soon as I shut the door behind me, she lunged at the doorknob. She was strong for her size and I had difficulty getting her hands off the door. All the while, she continued screaming a fit.

I guess when I heard the door open behind me, I expected it. I turned my head to see the biggest, nastiest guy that I'd seen yet on my trip. He was easily 6'2 and looked to be mid-30s, with a heavy muscular build and a bald white head. He was wearing boxers and a wife-beater tank top. His right arm was covered in tattoos and he had piercings in his lip and ears.

"Are you ok girl?" he asked looking at the girl hanging on the doorknob. He looked a little confused, at least he realized she was trying to get back in, not out, but I was worried at his attention to her, hoping I didn't run into a badass Captain-save-a-ho.

She dropped from the door and backed a little way down the hall toward him.

"No, he's mother fucker! He hit me!" she yelled.

The man glared at me, to which I responded with an eye roll.

"Man, this is just a dispute over the bill," I said to him.

"FUCK YOU!" screamed the girl as she lunged at me throwing slaps and attempting to dig her nails into my arms.

"Woh hoo! She's a feisty one!" said the man, now cracking a smile.

I would have appreciated some help even more, but it was enough that he didn't decide to come to the aid of a damsel in distress. That probably would have ended badly for me.

Fear began to build in my gut. If she was just a bargirl and acting this way, I'd simply figure out a way to throw her ass to the curb, but she said she was 17, if anyone besides a tattooed Westerner ended up involved, I could easily end up in a much worse spot. She certainly didn't seem afraid to lob accusations at me, and her screaming didn't seem like it would stop anytime soon.

"Ok ok ok!" I yelled at her. "I will give you more money, but only downstairs, and only if you shut the fuck up!"

"Ah man," smirked the bald wrestler, "Don't give in, this is fun."

Yea, thanks fucker.

She calmed down a little, but didn't relent completely, "Pay now mother fucker!"

Not seeing any other good options, I took out 500 baht and gave it to her, and said, "Ok, I will give you 1,000 more downstairs if you shut up."

She continued her scowl at me but thankfully turned toward the elevator.

"Ah ha ha ha," laughed the man. "You made out good didn't you girly?"

It was finally somewhat peaceful as we waited for the elevator and once again she dropped to her knees and went for my pants. I could only think, 'holy shit, the girl is fucking insane.'

"1,000 baht, I smoke you," she said.

I kept slapping her hands away, and when the elevator arrived, she continued grabbing at my pants. I moved in and she followed.

"Don't you want smoke?" she asked.

In what is probably the action that kept me out of jail, I reached into my pocket and pulled out the 1,000 baht and waved it at her.

"Here. Only if you let go," I said.

With the 1,000 baht in hand, she stood up and turned away from me as the door to the bottom floor opened and she walked out. I stood at the door to watch her walk toward the lobby when 2 of the condo security guards appeared. My eyes opened wide and nervousness shot through my body. She didn't flinch though, she casually moved to the side and kept walking.

I dropped back into the elevator and tried frantically to get the door closed.

I didn't make it.

The two guards filed into the elevator with me, one of them acknowledging me with a "Kop[11]."

He looked at the buttons and noticed my floor pressed and looked at me suspiciously, but then turned his head to wait for the doors to close.

I knew they'd eventually figure it out that I was involved in the disturbance, but I thought I'd wait until the girl had enough time to leave the premises. If she wasn't still here, this would just be a slap on the wrist for making too much noise.

"What's up guys?" I asked cheerfully.

Blank looks.

"Ok, sir?" one asked.

Neither of them spoke any English I surmised. I relaxed... and breathed a sigh of relief these guys didn't show up in time. I would have been at a severe disadvantage if that nutty girl could speak Thai to these guys while I could not be understood at all.

The guards exited the elevator first and looked down the hall and then stopped and spoke to each other in Thai before continuing behind me. By their tones, they were confused, maybe they were deciding if they should go right back down or wait around. As I got to my door, the guards had stopped at another door a couple down from mine, probably the one that called them.

---

[11] Like saying "hey."

I closed the door behind me and waited at the door listening. I heard the guards' voices and a Thai lady for a minute or two until her door closed and it was quiet.

I fell to the couch and stared at the ceiling for hours it seemed. I couldn't believe I got myself in that situation before I had even set foot out of the condo, but as I thought more about it, some of the events were puzzling to me. The first and most obvious was that she told me her age of 17. Why would she do that? If she actually was 17 and looking for work, surely she would have said 18. Or are there guys out there who would actually want to fuck her more if she said 17? In any case, I began to wonder if that age was true.

The only way she manages to blackmail me for 2,000 baht is because she said she was 17. If she said 18, I would have tossed her out of the condo and I wouldn't have given two fucks who was woken up in the process, at least not enough to pony up money to hush her up.

Just how well rehearsed was that little blackmail, I wondered. She was bat-shit crazy, that was obvious, but had she practiced that little routine a few times? If so, how would she have acted if I had given her money for sex?

After hours of analyzing, I finally concluded she was just fucking nuts and drunk and went ape shit on me due to the pressures of making money as a whore in Pattaya. Then I thought maybe a ladyboy wouldn't have been so bad.

5

A Tinder Success

Being involved in a crazy situation in a foreign country doesn't usually instill a ton of confidence. It was two days before I even left my condo again, thankfully I had some snack food to survive on while I hid away from the world. The whole time I was expecting Thai police to show up with the crazy girl and that evil scowl on her face pointing, "That's him!"

It was 11 AM when I took the step outside and made my way to the elevator. As luck would have it, a condo door opened behind me and I looked back to see that gigantic boxer punk who had stood and ridiculed me for giving away more money. He was again wearing some gym shorts and a white wife-beater tank top, I wondered if he had any other clothes.

I stopped before the elevators and waited for him. When he noticed me, his face livened up. He seemed like a cheery fellow anyway.

"Hey mate, where's your girlfriend?" he asked in a thick Australian accent.

"Did that amuse you?" I asked him.

"That made my night," he said. "I can't believe you gave her more money, she was already out the door."

"I didn't want to wake up everyone in the building, and did you see the guards come up?" I asked him.

"Ah, mate, don't worry about the guards here, they give fuck all about these girls," he said. "I've lived in this building for a year now, the guards have the residents' backs every time."

For some reason, I had trouble believing him. Sure, even in Thailand, prostitutes would be in the lowest class of citizens, but foreigners exist in a separate system. I'm sure the guards would have been on my side... for a few hundred baht. That price would be a few thousand if they found out she was 17.

"Well, thanks man, for not jumping in on her side when she accused me of hitting her," I said.

"Ah, no worries, mate. Some of these Thai girls are crazy bitches. I could tell right away she probably deserved to be hit anyway," he answered as we stepped into the elevator.

"I'm Nate," I said.

"Ben... cheers mate," he replied. "I'm going to the food court at Soi Buakhao, come along. So, tell me, how much did you end up giving that crazy bitch?"

On the way to the food court, I relayed the whole story to him, including the part about her saying her age was 17. Ben didn't really strike me as the judgmental do-gooder.

"So, do you think she was really 17?" I asked him.

"Fuck mate, she was probably younger. I don't remember seeing any bumps on her body at all. These Thai girls get to working at 14. You know what I would have done? I would have fucked that hateful bitch until she wanted to change careers, and if she asked for more than 1000 baht, I'd have tossed her skinny ass off the balcony," he said. "She's not going to involve the police, mate. She's not supposed to be hooking."

I wondered how much of Ben's Bravado was real. It's certainly true that many disrespectful and arrogant men come to Thailand in order to treat women like trash. It's usually ingrained in them in some way. When in their home country, they will lie and seduce in any way they can just to get their dick inside a new pussy. It tends to cause a lot of stress in their life and they come to Thailand to seek an easier way. They'll still lie and take advantage of women while in Thailand, but it comes with fewer repercussions.

Of course, there are men everywhere who talk a big game when it comes to women, but who are actually respectful to women. A big guy like Ben, I would suspect to fall into this category and he's simply formed a habit of talking big and exaggeration, because hey, it's just not often anyone has the balls to call him out.

He was not the kind of guy I'd normally keep company with. Besides his mind-numbing arrogance, he was the type of guy who'd get me into trouble. I'm not a big guy like him, and while he's acting out somewhere, it'd probably be me that gets the aggressive attention.

We had a nice little chat on the way to the Soi Buakhao food court, and it was comforting to have some company after the rough start to my trip. He was dismissive of my stories as well, telling me I was just unlucky and that I'd find all the great pussy I wanted in Pattaya. By the time we sat down to eat, I was feeling much better.

The food court at Soi Buakhao was a collection of stalls with rock-bottom prices. There were foods ranging from fried crickets to hamburgers and French fries and of course all the Thai food you could dream of. Ben teased me a bit about trying the crickets, but I passed. I'd assume if you deep fried an ashtray, it'd be edible, but why bother?

Ben headed straight to a beer stall to pick out a Singha, while I found a soda and again got teased a little.

"It's not even noon," I said.

"What tha fuck you in Thailand for then?" he countered.

"Not to get wasted. I'm here to fuck my brains out. I'm not young like you, my dick doesn't work quite as good," I said.

That was probably not true, I'd bet my dick worked every bit as well as his. Ben seemed to be one of those sex tourists that is more into the booze than the sex. *Or so I thought.*

Ben told me to stay away from the "quasi-Western" food at the food court, which suited me just fine. We ordered from what seemed to be the nicest Thai stall and I ate green chicken curry and a papaya salad. I told them to make it number 2 spicy, but it wasn't spicy enough for me. Afterwards I always ordered 3 spicy, which was too spicy. The scale was 1-10 and even 3 burned my tongue and throat for up to an hour after eating. As for Ben? 0 spicy.

It was decent food, well worth the 200 baht I paid for the two meals and a soda. Maybe coming to the food court was not such a bad idea.

Never barfine a friend's favorite girl.

"So, I'm going to a bar to see a little honey. Want to come? You can't be a pussy and not drink though," Ben asked.

I didn't have a better idea at the time, so I agreed and he led me down a nearby street back towards Second Road. We passed a long row of beer bars, most of which were closed until we came to a small one titled "British Bar." It and one next door seemed to be doing a nice business in that early afternoon. There was a half dozen or so... well... British-looking bar patrons. I felt strange being two colonials walking up.

It seemed a friendly little place, a square bar with 6 seats on each of the sides with one lonely pool table. As we approached, my jaw dropped at the cutest little girl walking up to Ben. She was wearing a tight black and white striped one-piece dress with flat shoes showing her height at barely 5 foot. She was slim and attractive with jiggly boobs and a nice bubble butt. Her jet-black hair was pulled into a ponytail, showing her wide cheekbones and tanned skin, probably from working all day in this exposed bar. It was her smile though, she had a cheerful, happy smile that probably lightened up everyone around her. Her age seemed about 20.

"Hey, honey," she said to Ben.

She casually walked up to Ben and wrapped her arms around his waist, about as high as she could reach. I assumed this was a daily visit. It seemed strange to me with all the bluster he gave me the whole morning that he'd have loyalty to a particular girl at a beer bar, but that seemed to be the case.

"This is my mate, Nate," he said.

"Hey, sexy man!" said the girl and gave me a hug. "I'm Porn[12]."

Porn was the sweetest, most loveable girl I'd met so far on the trip. That may not say much, but I assure you she was an amazing girl. I was smitten the moment I felt those mushy tits rub against my belly. I would have tried to barfine her on the spot if she wasn't Ben's girl. I have some

---

[12] Porn – pronounced more like "Pone"

rules concerning sex trips. There are thousands of girls in Pattaya or any sex destination, and while jealousy over a sex worker is stupid, no one ever said sex tourists were smart men. There is no reason to move in on another man's favorite girl, it will only cause problems. Never barfine a friend's favorite girl.

The three of us sat down at the bar and I begrudgingly ordered a San Mig Lite, while Ben went with the Singha. Ben also ordered a drink for Porn, soda water.

I liked the little British bar. The other guys sitting at the bar were friendly enough, most of them my age or older, with Ben the youngest. There were a couple of other girls hanging out, both dog ugly compared to Porn. They were sizing me up as the fresh blood, and I tried not to make eye contact. An attentive mama-san/bartender ran things from the middle of the bar.

I didn't know it yet, but that little British Bar would become a regular afternoon hangout for me on the trip and I would end up drinking way more than I intended and doing things that didn't really seem like myself. Something in me started to change as I drank those San Mig Lites on a hot February afternoon in Pattaya, flirting but trying not to show it with a gorgeous young bargirl busy hanging on a brut of a man who seemed like would become my friend.

Ben was truly at home in the bar, he was relaxed and friendly with everyone. "Cheers mate" and "Thanks mate" seemed to be heard every 5 minutes. Another man at the bar who was three sheets to the wind when we arrived conversed with him on everything from world politics to bargirl love. His name was Bob, though everyone called him "Farang Bob" as if the description was necessary. He was a 45-year-old Brit with a naturally bald head and like Ben wearing a wife beater. He was almost Ben's size but seemed to be no longer keeping up with the gym as he had that saggy appearance.

They struck me as exactly the kind of guys I loathe hanging out with on a sex vacation. They were drunks, pure and simple, it was the bar scene they really enjoyed. They came to Thailand to get loaded and stay that way, the pussy was a bonus. I should have had my beers and never came back.

"Meet, fuck?"

It was a simple message that rolled across my phone from Tinder about five beers into my afternoon binge. It was from a girl I'd matched with the night before but who had not responded to my first messages.

Her name was Suda. Her pictures on Tinder were undoubtedly female, though she did list herself as "100% girl" for good measure. She was a cutie. She looked about 25, with a slim sexy body. She had short brown dyed hair and small lips.

I flipped through the pictures and showed them to Ben.

"Damn mate, she's hot. You are going to go fuck her now?" he asked.

"I think so," I replied. "Do you think she really looks like that?"

I was a little apprehensive about meeting another girl from Tinder.

"Ha. Think she's a ladyboy?" he asked.

I had not mentioned my little post-op experience to Ben yet.

"She certainly doesn't look like one," I said.

"Go for it, mate."

He was right, I should go for it. I texted her back that I was at the BASE and would meet her in the lobby.

"1,000 baht, ok?" was her answer.

That seemed too good to be true if she was the girl in the pictures, but I was going to find out and settled my tab at the bar.

"I want to go check out this girl," said Ben. "And if she's a boy, I'll help you beat his ass."

So, the two of us walked the short distance back to the condo and had a seat in the lobby and waited for Suda to arrive.

As we sat in the lobby, we did what guys usually do when they are sitting in public and have nothing to do – talk about the women all around. The condo was busy that late afternoon. There were single girls who looked like sex workers, single girls who looked like normal girls, groups of girls, groups of guys and girls. We had quite the time with our little judgments.

"Oh, this one's gotta be yours," laughed Ben.

An older hag in a tight black dress which constricted her fatty belly jumped off the back of the scooter outside and headed toward the condo. We were still laughing as she entered the lobby and glanced at us.

"Oh yea, she wants you," laughed Ben clearly loud enough for her to hear.

Ben had no shame whatsoever.

Then a couple of obvious ladyboys appeared and entered the lobby.

"Right here!" yelled Ben. "Here's the one you are looking for!"

I slouched in my chair.

"Oh, really, sexy man!" yelled back one of them, as they stopped for a second.

"He's joking, move along," I yelled. "Alright, knock it off."

Ben burst out into laughter, and I did too after a moment. I was terrified at the prospect of having a ladyboy in my vicinity again, but I quickly lightened up.

Ben cooled down the hollering at ladyboys at least, or maybe there were just no more to holler at, and I began to enjoy those 15 minutes in the lobby playing the judgmental foreigners. Sometimes, you just have to let loose and be a jerkoff.

"Woh, check that one out, mate," said Ben calling my attention to a girl that appeared across the driveway walking in from the street.

She had a tall slender figure wearing a tasteful green evening dress. She had shoulder-length brown hair and moved with confidence.

"Oh my God, that's her," I said.

"No fucking way," Ben replied.

I stood up to open the door for her and to get a good look at her face. It was definitely her, I felt I had hit the jackpot.

"Nathan?" she asked, smiling and showing a perfect set of white teeth.

"Uh huh."

"I'm Suda," she said and entered the lobby and stopped to wait for me.

"This is my friend, Ben," I said.

Ben was standing behind me with the biggest grin on his face. I could only think, 'please don't say something completely inappropriate.'

"So, you want to do us both at the same time?" he asked her.

So much for that.

Before she could have a chance to process the question, I said, "He's joking. He's my friend across the hall, and he will STAY across the hall."

Suda merely giggled.

"Gay," said Ben.

Besides that I didn't know Ben well enough to get naked with him, this girl was gorgeous, I wanted her all to myself for an hour or so.

The three of us got in the elevator and we were both drooling over her. She didn't seem to mind.

"So, you ever been to this condo?" I asked.

"Yes, a few times," she answered. "It is nice place."

"Do you only work in Tinder?" I asked.

"Yes," she said.

"Do you take it in the bum?" Ben interjected.

Suda shook her head calmly.

I was ready to get free of Ben's company. This was not the side of Ben I saw at the bar with Porn.

After we arrived at our floor and headed down the hall, Ben stopped at his condo.

"When you are done with her, send her over," said Ben.

Suda turned to him and smiled.

"I don't know, your friend nicer than you," she said.

"I'll be nice honey," Ben said and watched us walk the distance to my condo.

Sharing girls with friends is not something I'm fond of. While Suda meant nothing, if it became a habit of sharing girls with Ben, eventually one of them would mean something. And then there was the matter of comparing dicks and other kinds of sexual performance. Many girls are drama queens and would live for causing rifts between customers. Of course, there was always the possibility Ben was an asshole and would drive a good girl away from both of us.

"Don't wear her out, mate. Save some for me," he said.

Finally, the door was closed and I was out of the company of the boisterous Ben, and one-on-one with the beautiful young Suda. There was something about Suda, I knew this was going to be a good experience and lacking any negative surprises. She was calm and confident and not in a rush.

"How long have you been in Pattaya?" she asked.

"I just got here," I answered.

"Oh! You looking girlfriend?" she giggled. "How long you stay?"

"A month."

"Ok, I stay with you," she said.

"Boom boom first," I said.

She giggled.

"I need to take a shower, I've been drinking all day," I said to her.

"Ok, I wash you."

Suda began to take charge of our encounter at that point. After I started the shower, she helped me take off my clothes, even batting away my hands as I tried to do it myself. So, I stood in my tiny bathroom letting her disrobe me. I had a cheesy smile on my face. It was a long time coming to get the service I was looking for in Thailand.

As she dropped my shorts to the floor, my dick sprung out erect, and she slid her hands over it as she stood up.

"Oh, very big," she said.

I smirked. Unlike my first encounter, that comment meant nothing to me, just something a working girl must say. I wondered if when Ben got the same comment, he would believe it? He'd likely stand proud and answer, "I know baby."

Suda backed off and began undressing. She lifted her one-piece dress over her head revealing her skinny body with only small cotton panties underneath. I love skinny legs, they were her best feature, though her flat belly and little pointy nipples also fueled my desire. I suspected she'd had a baby, as her tits drooped slightly in that motherly way, though her body was free of stretch marks.

She pulled her hair into a ponytail and followed me into the small condo shower.

"Oh, sexy man!" she said as she began lathering me up. I don't really believe that one either but I love hearing it.

I could not keep my hands off her in the shower, I pulled her skinny body into me and ran my hands down her back and over her small ass. My hands glissaded across her smooth skin feeling the form of her ass and finding their way to her little asshole. She began to sway her hips as my hand danced between her ass and pussy.

With her hands, she was slowly massaging my cock and balls with a heavy amount of soap with so little room between us that the head of my dick was bouncing off her soft stomach.

I looked into her eyes and lowered my mouth to hers, wondering if she'd kiss me. She did. She kissed me with playful smooches and sticking her tongue out to massage mine. I was losing my mind. The contrast between her and my earlier encounters relieved me. I sucked her tongue passionately.

She chuckled.

"Ok, honey, let's go bed," she said.

Not allowing me to dry myself, she toweled me off while we stood naked in the bathroom. She started with my hair and thoroughly dried my body all the way down. After she finished with my feet, she was kneeled on the floor with my erect penis just above her head. She looked at it and giggled.

Then she dropped the towel on the floor and pushed her face into my dick kissing the underside of it while looking into my eyes. She continued this tease for half a minute or so when she let the tip of it slide into her mouth and then back out.

"Oh God," I said. "Let's get to the bed!"

She giggled more and stood up, kissed me, and toweled herself off.

Getting to the bedroom, I collapsed on my back and Suda collapsed on my crotch. She started at first with the same teasing as in the bathroom, and finally braced her hands on my hips, took me in her mouth, and began bobbing madly.

I relaxed and watched the girl go to work. I liked this kind of blowjob, the kind where the girl doesn't touch my dick with her hands. The only part of her on my dick was her lips and tongue. Her mouth was fully lubricated and slid up and down with a tiny bit of suction keeping my dick enveloped in her mouth.

As she worked it more and more, she began to take me deeper. I could feel the head of my dick impacting the back of her throat. This girl loved to suck cock. Though not uncommon, it's certainly not all sex workers that enjoy that part of the service, such as my massage girl on Soi 13. When I meet a cocksucker, I tend to push it as far as she is willing to go.

"You love sucking dick, don't you?" I asked.

"Mmmhmm," came the muffled answer.

My deviant mind cycled through the possibilities, finally coming up with one of my favorites, though rarely acceptable positions.

"Come here, honey, lay down on the bed, like so," I said to her.

I positioned her laying on her back across the bed with her head slightly hanging off the side. The whole time I gauged her reaction and well, the big smile and excitement told me I had no need to hold back.

I stood over her head and bent my knees slightly so my dick pointed toward her mouth. She stuck out her tongue and let it slide inside. With one hand, I grabbed a tit for balance and with the other, I reached forward and slid a finger over her clit. Her skinny legs were now splayed out sideways. It was a sexy sight.

All I could see of her head was the bottom of her chin as I began working my thrusts into her mouth faster and faster. So far, she was a good sport.

When she reached both her hands around to my ass, that seemed like a signal that I could go further. At the end of my thrusts, when I felt my dick in the back of her throat, I began making a deeper push. In her neck, I could see my dick opening her throat. So far, she showed no signs of gagging or backing off, though I felt her tensing up.

I stopped playing with her clit and grabbed both her tits for more leverage. Then I thrust deep into her throat watching it expand in her neck and then I held my dick there. Her body went rigid, and I could sense her discomfort but she didn't move besides some tiny repositioning in her head.

Finally, she flinched. A gag erupted in her throat around my dick and she grabbed my hips to push me off.

I pulled completely out and she turned her head to the side and finished her gag. Then dutifully positioned her head back in place and wiped the spit from her mouth.

"You ok?" I asked.

By that I really meant, *can I go again?*

"I'm ok," she said and opened her mouth and stuck her tongue back out.

Wow, what a sport.

I repeated some gentle thrusts until time to gag her again. This time, I reached between her legs and slid a finger in a soaked pussy to pull her body into my dick as I pushed. I managed the entire shaft of my cock all the way in her throat, and her neck bulged.

She didn't last but a second before her whole body convulsed. I held my dick in her throat through one gag as saliva ran down the sides of her head, but on the second, her body twisted in an attempt to get free, so I pulled out.

She turned on her belly and I was afraid she was going to vomit in the floor, but she recovered and even turned back over ready to take more, though I could see in her face she was apprehensive. I thought the girl had had enough.

"That was awesome," I said.

"You are bad," she said, smiling a little.

Seeing that I was ready for sex, she moved up to the pillows laying on her back.

"You have condom?" she asked.

Again with that question.

Since she didn't come with a purse, I assumed she didn't have one. Momentarily, I thought about claiming not to have one, and perhaps looking back on it, I should have done that just to see what would have happened, but she seemed like an experienced enough girl that a condom was probably a good idea. Though, not so experienced as to bring her own condoms? That's one thing I'll never understand about Asian sex workers.

Suda loved having my dick inside her. The look in her face was one of pure sexual lust. That bit of face fucking must have turned her on madly, or she deserved an academy award. She pulled on my hips until I was bouncing on her pussy with all my weight and with all the speed I could manage. Within half a minute, I was dripping sweat.

Finally, I had her switch to doggy style so I could slam into her with less effort. She braced her hands against the wall and pushed back against me. This girl loved sex, and I wish I could have lasted longer. After I finished, I fell face first to the bed, finally feeling satisfied with a sexual encounter in Pattaya. Suda draped a leg and arm over me, holding me for a time.

"Good job," she said. "I liked it."

Wait until I face fuck you next time.

Suda showed no impatience in leaving as we lay in bed, and I began planning my next encounter with her already. She was likely the kind of professional that sought regular business instead of churning through as many customers as possible, and my initial thoughts were to become a regular customer. If she was that much fun on the first short time session, I'd imagine an entire night would have been a blast. Finally, she got up and started getting dressed.

"Ok, thank you honey, you text me anytime," she said.

She had never asked for money, and the thought of cold-shouldering her by giving her only the 1,000 baht she asked for never crossed my mind. I picked through my wallet and gave her 1,500, which I thought was too low considering that's how much the post-op got, but then again, I saw no need to be overly generous.

"Which condo your friend?" she asked.

At this point, I remembered Ben's comment to 'send her over.' *Ugh.*

The thoughts I had of becoming a regular customer evaporated as I could not abide the thought of sharing her with Ben. Why? I don't know, it was some strange stupid ego, or maybe I didn't want to have my lips anywhere close to her mouth, now knowing she would likely be deep throating Ben in a few minutes.

I walked her out of the condo and pointed out his door. As I watched that slender figure mosey down to Ben's door, I couldn't help but laugh at myself and my jealous emotion. I wondered if it existed at all in Ben.

6

Devil's Threesome

"Damn mate, that girl was a freak!" Ben exclaimed to me sitting at the British Bar for another afternoon drunk.

I quickly got the story that Suda gagged on Ben's dick as well, though it seemed like he was a bit nicer than I was, not turning her upside down on the bed to gain leverage. I didn't relay that part of it to him, didn't want to give the big man any ideas.

"Mate, we should call her back some time and do her at the same time. I'll fuck her from behind while she blows you!" Ben laughed. "Maybe she'll give us a discount. 600 baht each!" *Stingy fuck.*

Ben seemed giddy as if she was the first nympho whore he'd ever had. I had nearly forgotten about her. She was great fun for sure, but not the kind of thrill I look for on sex vacations. I enjoy making a connection with a girl before shoving my dick in her throat. Meeting up from an online dating service and then sharing with my new friend across the hall was a little too impersonal for me.

Porn showed up at the bar.

"Hey, Sexy men!" she screamed.

"Hello, my love!" replied Ben. "We go boom-boom this afternoon?"

Porn was an oddity. She was a young beautiful girl bused in from Isaan to work in the bars but clung to her desire not to screw every foreigner with eyes on her. I found it pathetic that Ben and Farang Bob visited this bar nearly every day to drool over her in some belief that someday maybe she'd go fuck them.

Not that I couldn't see the attraction. She was an amazing girl. She carried herself with the grace of a runway model and interacted with everyone, from locals to foreigners, with the charisma of a successful real estate agent.

She always wore a tight dress with black and white stripes. She spent her entire day lounging around that little bar, drinking watered-down cocktails for commission and tips, and playing a miserable game of pool all the while seeming to enjoy every minute of it. I wanted to explain to her that a girl with her looks and personality could be doing so much more, although that is probably not what she wanted. She likely had a very simple desire, to marry a rich foreigner and get the hell out of Thailand. She was too smart for the ragtag duo of Farang Bob and Ben, who only wanted her pussy.

When I first discovered she was not apt to barfine, I lost interest, but the more time I spent at that bar, the more I developed a crush on her, same as my newfound friends. It was impossible not to.

"So, you spend all your time at this bar, but you've never barfined her?" I asked Ben when she stepped away to flirt with some other customers.

"Nah, mate. But she says she'll go with me someday."

"Are you fucking for real?" I laughed.

He glared at me.

"Well, I don't know. I guess if I actually lived here like you, I might devote the time, but Jesus Christ, there are so many bars without stuck-up girls in this city, I don't see what you'd bother."

"I come here for the booze, not for her," he said.

I didn't believe him. Sure, the bar was cozy and cheap, but there was only one reason to go there every day.

Farang Bob on the other hand... I doubted he pretended to be there for any other reason. In between the drags on his cigarettes, he stared mercilessly at Porn, his eyes following her every move. He was a big foreboding character, and I thought it had to make her uncomfortable, though I'm sure she enjoyed the funds he lavished on her drinks.

"My turn, honey!" he yelled at her after she finished with a small group of customers.

"Yes, ok!" yelled Porn.

She climbed on his knee and put her arm around his shoulders like she'd done it thousands of times. He wrapped both arms around her and started slurring in her face, while she smiled and pretended to enjoy it. Any onlookers could tell she was merely doing her job, while he may have felt she liked him. I wondered how often I'd been looked at by another sex tourist in the same way I was looking at Farang Bob.

"So, has she ever barfined with Farang Bob?" I asked Ben.

He laughed and shook his head.

"Has she barfined with anyone?"

"I don't know, mate. She's always here, every day until the bar closes."

As it were, the forbidden fruit was certainly making an impression on every man at that bar, including myself.

We wasted the afternoon at the British Bar, with typical sex tourist talk such as, "How often do you wear condoms?" and "Ever pissed on a girl?" you know, almost the same as office talk back home. *Almost.*

"Mate, my friend told me about this tramp at Bunny Bar on Soi 6. Supposedly, she'll do anything. Want to go rip up a butt hole?"

Well, I didn't have a better idea at the time.

Sleazy. It's a word that can be used to describe the entire city of Pattaya. Even the modern Central Mall in the heart of the city can exude sleaziness as one mingles with overweight 60-year-olds grabbing the ass of a young honey enjoying her all-expenses-paid shopping trip. You can run into sex shops anywhere, pick a random side street and start walking. You'll pass normal looking shops and condo buildings and then a girlie bar.

In that city of depravity, Soi 6 stands out. It is the city's tacky mecca of sex. The bars there cater more to the short-term barfine, with a couple floors of rooms directly above. There might be more used condoms flushed down the toilets in that dingy back alley in a 24-hour period than the whole of Beach Road. The entire street is one big lineup. Men strolling down the street are beset on both sides by bargirls sitting in front of their bars or at a small bar overlooking the street. The finer of the girls may be positioned standing in the middle of the street for enticement.

While the impersonal nature of Soi 6 did not appeal to me, Ben was at home. He would flirt with any girl to approach, copping as many free feels as he could, usually as I stood back and waited. I've never been into it. Perhaps I was trained at a young age not to touch, but I never saw the attraction in touching a woman just for the sake of the touch. It's as if Ben's day was defined by how much skin he could invade.

The girls varied in their reactions to him. Some saw his menacing groping paws as a threat and kept their distance, while others accepted the ass pats and belly caresses as necessary to win a customer.

Near Bunny Club, a particularly aggressive girl had Ben wrapped up. She wore a two-piece uniform showing a flat hard belly, but with skin coated in stretch marks. A cute 30-year-old face put her among the top lookers on the street.

"Honey, I do discount for you, fifteen hundred!"

"O' roight, let me see," Ben said.

As she clung to his waist, he slid his hand across her shorts, around her hips, and squeezed her ass cheek pulling her closer.

"Nice ass. Fifteen hundred in the bum?" he asked.

"You want anal?" she asked.

"Fuck yes!"

"Ok, I do anal three thousand five hundred."

"Oh my God!" said Ben.

His hand inched closer to the middle of her ass.

"You think you could take it?" he asked.

"No problem, honey!"

"You do us both anal, thirty-five?" asked Ben.

She looked at me. I rolled my eyes.

"No way, three thousand five hundred each! Not same time!"

"We're mates, we do together or not at all," Ben said.

"Crazy!" she said.

"It's ok or not?" Ben asked.

"Three thousand five hundred each. Same time ok."

I marveled at the prowess of Ben's handling of a hooker. I knew his goal was to find her boundaries, rather than striking a deal.

"You wish honey. Two thousand each, same time, final offer," said Ben.

"No anal, two thousand each," she said.

"What? You said fifteen hundred already!" Ben said.

"Fifteen, not same time!"

"That's fucking stupid."

Ben removed his arms. She continued hanging on his waist.

"Come on, fifteen each, same time, boom-boom pussy," she said.

"Ok, off you go," said Ben.

He pushed her waist down and her arms fell to her side.

"Three thousand each, anal!" she said.

"No," Ben said.

She rested her hands on her hips and scowled. I saw her considering the idea of letting us violate her ass for 4,000 baht. Truly didn't seem like a bad deal, these girls don't get that much for an hour's work too often. Most in the city don't, except the occasional masseuse on Soi 13 I suppose. I glanced at her as we continued our walk up Soi 6, waiting for her to chase us screaming her acceptance of the deal, but I guess she sold her ass more dearly.

"So, if she accepted 2,000 each from us?" I asked.

"I would have torn her ass open for you," he said.

"What a pal."

A short way later, we arrived at Bunny Club. Like most of the bars on the street, and the city, it was an open-air bar in a small storefront space. A few girls sat at the high street-facing tables, heads propped on their elbows, hating life.

One older girl in a red dress rose from a table in the bar to greet us as we entered. Inside, there was a long black bar on one side with more high tables in front and some sofas in the back. There were a few customers sitting at the bar, a few girls sitting in the back, but otherwise seemed dreary for Thailand.

"Where's Tik?!" boomed Ben.

The few ladies sitting around the bar craned their heads at the sudden commotion. I could sense a bit of frustration. Tik must get most of the business.

"Tik, she very busy. She come back later."

"Ok, we wait," said Ben.

"We have other girls, nice girls."

"Which ones do anal?"

"Ok, you wait for Tik."

For the next couple hours, we sat alone in the Soi 6 bar sucking down shots and beers and planning our assault. Just two sex tourists who got together to share a 3-holer prostitute. We were at home with the other drunks, usually fished from the street by the door girls, but who either glanced around and made their exit or sat down to have a beer, before moving on.

The waitress would flirt with us, but the other girls seemed to leave us alone as if they all knew we'd be spending money on none of them. Occasionally, we'd receive a giggle from one of our drunken antics, but otherwise, they had no time for us, since a paying customer could happen down the street any moment. Dreary bar indeed, it was more of a waiting room.

"Do you think she's coming back?" Ben yelled at the waitress.

"She always come back."

I would have thought two hours gone for a Soi 6 bargirl to be unusual. How much juice did her customer have? And it was becoming a problem.

"Ben, I'm fucked up," I said.

The bar was spinning, as I had kept pace the whole day.

Ben laughed in ridicule.

"Well, you don't have to be sober for what we're doing," he said.

"Well, fuck, unless she is hot as fuck, which I doubt, I ain't gonna be getting it up," I said.

Ben seemed to ponder an idea.

"Ah, damn, mate! Good thinking, I'll be right back," he said.

Ben hurried out of the bar, his labored steps revealing he was borderline trashed as well.

"Another shot?" asked the waitress.

I waved my hand and peered toward the street, squinting through the foggy eyes of an inexperienced drunkard. The street was lively, vehicle traffic was shut down and throngs of men went about their night. The bar swirled as I relaxed my elbows on the table, balancing my weight, and dreading when I'd have to move. For the moment, I was good, my existence wrapped around drunken thoughts, uncaring for the world going on around me. The image of Porn danced in my mind, her golden-brown neck, the curvature of her body, how I wanted to wrap my arms around her. If she was doing Ben and me, I could certainly perform. Then Suda's slender shape appeared. The scene of Ben and me standing over her as she coughed on our cocks. In my drunken dream, I was outperforming, she was peering at me as if the champion and pushing against Ben's rambling advances. Even the smelly massage girl popped in my head. I thought of entering her without a condom, those tight hips. I wondered how she would feel. My eyes drifted down to the bar and I urged myself back awake, but my drunken dream is where I wanted to stay.

When a fresh face walked in, I barely took notice. She was an older bargirl, as they go, maybe 28. A professional, no doubt, as if she'd strode into that bar thousands of times. Under her purple top and black miniskirt was the body of a woman who was beginning to let herself go but was still holding an appealing form. Skinny legs, skinny arms, but a touch of extra weight in the belly and the ass that was out of proportion to her small chest. Her heavily made-up face carried a confident smile under a mop of curled glitter-dusted hair. She wasn't a turn-off, but not one I'd pick.

As a waitress pointed her in my direction, my reality snapped back.

"Hi, you wait for me?" she asked, extending her polished hand.

"Uhh, I guess so," I said.

"How you know me?" she asked.

"My friend… he coming…"

"Buy me drink?"

"Suure."

"Where are you from?" she asked.

"America."

"How old are you?"

110

I felt like vomiting at the banality of the questions, or maybe it was the liquor. Either way, there were no beer goggles for her. I wasn't attracted to her in the slightest, and if she was introducing herself as a regular bargirl instead of one who took dick up the ass, my bed asleep seemed a much better option.

"Another drink? I need catch up to you!"

"Why not."

She sensed I wasn't attracted to her, but confidence shown through her personality. As we sat there making small talk about other girls, ladyboys, and Pattaya, she broke through my resistance. A true professional. She could sit there, smile, and drink all night despite the utter bore of a customer.

"How long have you been working here?" I asked.

"Oh, long time."

"How old were you when you started?"

"Eighteen."

"Always on Soi 6?"

"Yes, always."

"Never get married?"

Tik laughed.

"Many men want to marry me, but they so jealous. I love my job," she said.

"You love this job?" I asked.

"Very much, I love boom-boom."

I laughed. "So do I. I don't hear a lot of girls say that."

"Why not?" she asked.

"I don't know, you tell me. Why you love boom-boom?" I asked.

"Cause I love DICK!" she giggled. "I love fuck. I love men."

It was refreshing to hear a bargirl speak that way. I wondered how many dicks she'd had in her pussy her whole life. 10,000? 3 per day, 6 days a week, for 10 years? How many in her mouth? And, how many up her ass? Why did I feel less attraction to her because of her mileage? I'm not alone in that regard. Most men are more attracted to women who've been with fewer men. I suppose it makes sense if you are searching for a bride, though I couldn't put a rational reason on that either. When searching for a one-night stand, wouldn't it be a plus? Wouldn't you want a girl who had done it all before and would know how to make the experience better for you? I gathered Tik was one of those. So long as you treated her decent, she'd do her best to make sure you had a great time.

"I bet you've done some crazy things," I said.

"What you want?"

"What do you do?"

"Anyting you want, honey."

"That's what I heard."

"So, what you want?"

I paused.

Had I been there alone, I likely wouldn't have been speaking with Tik. If she had managed to lure me into buying her a drink, even sober, I'm not sure I'd be interested in anything with her. In that drunken state, I was only interested in the support the table was providing. How some guys drink to the point of slurring and stumbling and still follow their dick to any spread legs is beyond me. I get drunk, I pass out, end of story. Maybe I'm a lightweight, or any other of the judgmental names wasted tourists lob around, but I rarely do something I regret. *Usually.*

"Anal?" I asked.

"How much you pay?"

Her response instant, her expression businesslike, it was nothing for her to discuss payment over having a dick in her ass.

"Actually, my friend…"

Thank God for Ben's perfect timing. The beast strode back into the bar, plowing through bargirls and other customers as if he'd regained 100% of his motor skills. I nodded my head in Tik's direction.

"Oh, fucking finally, this the chick, huh? Honey, you ready for some fucking fun?" he asked, taking his seat at the table.

"Oh, hell yes, baby. My God, I think you hurt me, though!" Tik said.

Her face had brightened up, revealing excitement, no boring party for her.

"We want to fuck your ass hole. How about 4,000 baht?" Ben asked.

Straight to the point. Ben had negotiating with bargirls down to an art. He knew how to start low on bargirl haggling.

"My God, you are so big! Let me see!" Tik said. Her hands reached under the table to Ben's crotch.

She laughed. "What the fuck, you already hard!" She said as she began stroking.

"Ok, 4,000 each, with condom," she said.

Ben looked at me with frustration.

"No, 4,000 total," he said.

"Oh, fuck off, honey!" Tik said.

She seemed amused. There was no desperation in her voice like the girl on the street earlier. Though Ben may have inadvertently increased her price, I could see in her demeanor she would not take less than 4,000 baht for anal, and it wouldn't bother her in the slightest if she ended up with no customer.

"4,000 no condom?" asked Ben.

Wear a condom, dummy.

"You want fuck my ass bareback?"

"Fuck yes," Ben said.

"10,000 baht. You do anyting. Fuck my ass, fuck my mouth, cum inside. Anyting you want, honey."

Ben glared. His desire for that kind of experience ran deep, but I doubted a man who eats at the Soi Buakhao food park every day could cough up 10,000 baht. And were there any thoughts going through his brain like was going through mine? This aged prostitute, admittingly going through as many dicks as she could, offering bareback services in her ass. If she offered in her ass, she surely went bareback in her pussy for a lower price. The bargirls in Pattaya are tested, at least that's what they say. In reality, the extent of the tests and the enforcement of hiring is left mostly to the bars, which will vary widely. You aren't in a legally-regulated Nevada state brothel, you are in Thailand. Maybe she knows she already has something and doesn't mind giving it to you. She must make the money for the family while she still can, you know. Wear a condom, dummy.

"8,000?" Ben asked.

Tik grinned and leaned toward him, still stroking his crotch.

"8,000 each?" she asked.

I threw up a little in my mouth. The burn of mixed liquor, cheap beer, and stomach acid. I coughed and tried to wash it down as the two deviants, ecstatic at their agreed debauchery, chuckled.

"I'm not even paying 4,000, sorry," I said.

"8,000 for me, and he can take video," Ben said.

Laughter erupted from Tik.

"I'm porn star now?" she mocked.

"Ben," I said. "I need to pass out, I'm too fucked up. Can't hold a fucking phone. Can't fuck probably."

"Fuck off. You're my mate. I got you covered."

Ben pulled a packet out of his pocket, broke it open and reached his hand under the table.

In my hand, he placed a little blue pill[13]. I stared at it in my hand, my head still swirling. *Problem solved, I suppose.*

"Da fuck!" Tik yelled. "Let me see."

"Only dick juice," Ben said.

"Let me see," said Tik.

I didn't have a particular reason to hide it from her. I lifted my hand.

"Ah! Oh fuck! You fuck my ass with Va-gra!" she laughed.

"No," I said. "I only have 2,000."

I dropped the pill in my mouth and downed the rest of my beer.

Tik laughed.

Ben laughed in approval.

---

[13] Viagra is readily available in Pattaya, from pharamacies over-the-counter, as well as street vendors. Be safe, buy in a pharmacy, unlike Ben who grabbed it from a Thai on the corner of Soi 6 and Second.

Tik smirked at Ben and reached her hand back to his crotch.

"You want fuck my ass no condom? 9,000 and he fuck my pussy 2,000 *same same* time."

Ben and I looked at each other.

"Same same?" I asked.

"One my ass, one my pussy, together, same same."

Talk about double dipping. This girl knows how to profit.

Ben literally jumped from his seat.

"Let's do it! I need money!"

Tik's arm flew in the air pointing to the outside corner of the bar and an ATM.

Ben bolted away.

"Yah!" Tik yelled.

I sighed.

"You ok honey?"

"I hope so."

"So much fun honey!"

Ben sped back in, again mowing down other patrons.

"Let's jet the fuck out of here!"

"Yes, let's go!" yelled Tik.

She grabbed both our wrists and ushered us toward the back.

"Wait," said Ben. "My condo."

"What! No way!" said Tik. "We go upstairs."

"My condo is free and nice. You think we'll pay for a shitty room?"

"I want fuck now honey! It's ok, I pay."

Obviously, she wanted to get the money as soon as possible. In her mind, anything could happen between now and the condo. It's the only time in my mongering career that a bargirl provided a bed free of charge.

She guided us to a stairway after a short conversation with a mama-san, and into a small room on the 3rd floor. As short-time rooms go, I couldn't complain. The bathroom wasn't cramped, the wall-mounted air conditioner was already running, and the bed had new white sheets.

She closed the door behind us and turned to us with a wide grin for a sex worker who just arrived in her office.

"Oh, my sexy boys!" she said.

She grabbed both our crotches. Mine was still limp. She cupped my balls.

I glanced at Ben. He was obsessed. His eyes were predatory, as if focused on the prey he was ready to capture. His dick hard, Tik's hand worked it through his shorts. He moaned and leaned forward, pulling the smaller Tik into him.

So how long until the blue pill kicks in?

"Shower!" she said.

She backed away and pushed her skirt down revealing her naked lower half, a bald crotch, and tattoos on her quads, one a black flower and the other Buddha's head. She untied the front knot on her top and off it went too, showing us a firm pair of mounds over her saggy midsection. As I'd observed in the bar, not unattractive, though nothing I'd be excited about. She bounced to the shower, her flat butt bouncing with her steps. Her ass crack seemed short, somewhat unproportioned to her legs. *Ben is going to fit in there?*

"Come on!" she yelled.

We looked at each other, that uneasy feeling of being naked with a near-stranger for the first time. How would we compare?

"Let's do this shit," said Ben.

"This is fucking crazy man," I said.

"Damn straight."

It's impossible to be in that situation without the thought of dick size coming up. The big man stripped off his clothes confidently. I suspected a massive cock to pop out, though I had not thought of Tik's testing downstairs. She would not have let her ass be violated by a huge schlong I'm sure. She already knew what to expect. And when I caught sight of it, my manhood was intact. He was no larger than me. On my body, it would look average, but on his, it seemed minuscule. Though he had the better body overall for sure, I doubt Tik cared about that sort of thing.

"Come on, men!"

Tik had the shower nice and hot as we crammed into the bathroom. She held the showerhead in her hand and quickly soaped herself off, paying extra attention to her crotch and ass, smiling the whole time, as we stood watching. Then she hung it, soaped up her hands, and lathered my crotch down.

"Mmhmm," she moaned.

Then she did the same to Ben. It's as if she'd done this before.

She moved back and forth between us, soaping us down, and rinsing us off. We giggled at her and each other, his cock pointing straight into the room, and mine limping along void of juice. *Annoying*.

"My God! So big!" she said.

She yanked on Ben's dick, with all of us still dripping, then she dropped to her knees and took him her mouth. She bobbed furiously on it, his hips bouncing against her. She never winced.

Her hand grabbed me and tugged. I'd felt this before, when a working girl rushes me into the bed and I've yet to get excited, as if she could simply pull me hard. Sometimes works, sometimes doesn't. By my thinking, I was still 15 minutes away from the Viagra kicking in.

She turned toward me, replacing her mouth on Ben's cock with a hand. Her face turned from giddy to seductive. She stuck her tongue out and flicked the end of my dick.

"You want cum on my face?" she asked.

Bam.

That explosion of lust. That feeling we get as men when a woman turns us on. Blood rushed to my cock.

She took me in her mouth and pulled slowly with a mouth full of spit.

"Damn, I want to cum on your face too," said Ben.

Tik didn't respond, her mouth full.

"Fuck this, let's go," said Ben.

He left the room.

Tik didn't mind him. She put her hands on my hips and kept pulling me in her mouth, committed to bringing me fully erect. It didn't take long.

I exited the bathroom refreshed and hard. Ben laid on his back on the bed.

Tik went to her purse and produced a packet of lube and a single condom.

I lay down beside Ben. Our dicks poked into the room at roughly the same size as Tik readied herself at the end of the bed with lube in her pussy and an open condom.

She crawled between my legs and rolled the condom over me, her face poised.

"Dude, you sure about this?" I asked.

"Fuck yes," said Ben.

"Let's fucking rock this bitch then," I said.

Tik giggled.

She climbed on and slid my dick in her, humping me slowly and motioning to Ben to get behind. She grabbed the lube and reached to her asshole. The girl knew what she was doing.

Ben climbed on the bed from behind and his hairy knees spread into my legs. Yep, rubbing legs with a man while fucking a whore.

He grabbed his dick and began to push it toward her ass.

Crash.

I suddenly had the weight of two bodies on me but even worse was the poking of Ben's dick I felt on my balls and covered shaft. So that's what it feels like, a hard tube of skin, poking around. Thank God I was still piss drunk.

I laughed. It was better than crying. Ben didn't seem to notice.

"Oh, for fuck's sake, this isn't going to work," said Ben, lifting himself.

"Wait, honey."

Tik put her hand on my shoulder balancing herself, not the most comfortable position for me, as she grabbed Ben's dick and pulled it toward her asshole. His knees pushed forward into my inner thighs. I spread my legs as much as possible, not really to assist him, more to keep him from rubbing me, but it seemed to help. I hoped he didn't get in too far, his knees were frighteningly close to my nuts.

"Eww," said Tik.

Ben smirked.

"Oh yea, there."

Ben grabbed her shoulders and pushed.

"Ow wee!"

"You like that honey?" Ben asked.

Tik lurched her body against our cocks like the pro she was. I was amazed at her movements. Her pussy was moving up and down on my shaft as Ben plowed in. She'd drop her weight the moment I was about to plop out. I began to enjoy it, I played with her nipples and watched the grimace on her face, turning from pleasure to pain depending on the momentum of Ben's thrust.

Then my eyes caught Ben's stare at me. Was he doing that the whole time? He looked happy. Like a bucket list item was being checked off and he was thrilled to be enjoying it. Though I couldn't join in his visual embrace. It felt too much like I was the one getting fucked and he was the one doing it. I hope I never get closer than that to knowing what it feels like.

It was not a quick Devil's Threesome. We went at it for a good 20 minutes, a few plop-outs, and a change of position. In the end, we decided we couldn't cum that way and the offer of cumming on her face seemed the best way to end things.

So, Ben fucked her ass while she sucked me off.

"You almost there?" Ben asked.

"No."

"How about now?"

"No."

"Da fuck, mate, I can't wait forever."

"Nine thousand Baht and you want to get it over with?"

"Woh wee honey! My ass hurt, cum now."

I helped myself along with my hand, the Viagra was slowing things down, as I'm not a regular user.

"Tell me when, I'm ready."

I stroked myself as Tik's mouth locked the tip of my dick, and announced when I was on the verge. Ben thrust hard a few times and then pulled out. Tik flipped to her back and looked into our eyes, mouth open, enthusiastic. She really loved it. She flicked her tongue. Of course, that's what I'd aim for.

Ben's dick was red and coated in lube with one tiny granule of shit at the base, an awful sight. He didn't seem to care.

Ben climaxed first the moment he got to her face with a manly "ugh!" I swear he was aiming for her eye socket. It squirt across her forehead and ran off her cheek. A drop in her eye, but she watched me through the other.

I finally released, shoving my dick to her lips. She flicked her tongue on the end as I dripped mostly in her mouth.

She didn't swallow. Ben and I crashed to the bed. Tik skipped off to the bathroom on cleanup duty.

"What's next, mate?" Ben asked.

I sighed and passed out. I don't remember getting home.

7

Clingy Massage Girl

I needed a break from the booze.

I've never been much of a drinker. To lose myself the way I had the last several nights was disconcerting. Something went wrong. For sure, I enjoyed every minute of it, but I would have enjoyed it just the same being a little soberer, though maybe the crossing of swords wouldn't have happened.

At least my jet lag was cured. I slept soundly after my three-way tryst, waking at the perfect time of noon. Ben had already messaged me for our daily trip to the food court. In fact, he had messaged me three times.

"Hey mate, ready to eat?"

"Yo!"

"Guess you are still passed out, meet me later at bar."

I didn't bother for a response as I'm sure I would be at the bar later. When traveling alone, it's nice to find other solo travelers to spend time with. If I could have chosen a more laid-back and less wasted person than Ben, I would have, but he was a good guy to have around for the experience.

I decided to have lunch by myself at Kiss Restaurant, a cheap spot next to my condo for people watching, and then cruised down Soi Honey to see if I could score a cheap massage plus boom-boom. Soi Honey had a few sex shops similar to Soi 13. I'd used one of them and wanted to try it out.

Continuing down Soi Honey from Second Road, I first passed salons, laundry shops, and short time hotels before reaching Honey Body Massage. Then the street changes to more of a red-light feel. The first to call at me was a ladyboy on the left manning one of the massage parlors. Pass. I was done with dicks for the trip.

Getting to the end of the street where it intersects with Soi Buakhao is where the fun is. On the right is a string of shops labeled as massage parlors, but the girls wearing evening dresses and arrayed out so the passers have a good view of them make no secret of the real service. One of the girls was holding a sign that clearly stated your options all the way to boom-boom. I wondered if I'd even get a massage.

Every day previously when I had passed with Ben, there were attractive ladies out front, but not today. I was bummed. I guess they were inside servicing some cock already, or perhaps simply taking the day off. Sex workers are fickle.

"Hey you, you come with me!" screamed a girl as she grabbed my arm to pull me toward a shop.

"No, I don't think so."

She was dog ugly… and obviously desperate.

It took a good minute to break her grasp. She was a strong chubby girl. I made every effort not to be too physical with her but finally yanked my arm away, causing her to lose balance and collapse to the ground.

"Fuck you!" she said.

"Well, fuck you, too!" I yelled back.

All the other girls looked at me as if I was the biggest douche to walk down the street. I wondered how I could have dealt with that better. I guess tenderness goes out the window for me at about 60 seconds when I'm being yanked on.

I got to the corner of Soi Honey and Buakhao and looked around at the dismal selection. The parlor on that corner is known as one of the best places to go for a quickie with an attractive girl, but at this moment, it was lacking, so I began a stroll down Soi Buakhao toward the food court.

Nearly at the food court, I spotted a massage parlor with blacked out windows and several girls sitting out front. They weren't in dresses though, they were wearing uniforms of blue striped shirts and jean shorts. I wondered what that meant. Not the same skirted uniforms of most massage parlors, but a uniform nonetheless. The shop didn't have the glass windows of most "legitimate" massage parlors, but if the girls weren't wearing provocative outfits like Soi Honey, I doubted sex would be on offer. Probably a scam joint, I surmised.

But my eyes were drawn to a tiny girl sitting out front playing with her phone, though before I could approach her, she got up and disappeared inside, giving me a great view of her backside. She had a sexy round bubble butt sitting on a small petite frame with skinny legs. By far the best option I'd seen this morning and I decided to give it a shot.

I made a beeline for the parlor and immediately the girls sitting around jumped to their feet. I guess it was a free-for-all on farangs and whoever grabbed the farang first got the business, and I found myself with another chubby girl latched onto my arm.

"Hey handsome, you want massage? Two girls? Only 500 baht," she said.

No for fuck's sake... No chubs.

I'm sure that was a good deal for her though. A man may not mind a chubby girl along with a cute one for the massage. Though I wouldn't pay 500 baht for an hour massage even with four girls.

The inside of the parlor had a small room with a tall counter and an old Thai lady behind it.

"Hello sir, you want big room?" she asked.

Two girls. Big room. This place was designed to extract as much as possible from foreigners. I've run across many places like it in travels. I looked behind the desk to see the little girl sitting on a couch still playing with her phone.

"I want her," I said.

She looked up, smiled and chuckled, and her face livened up with the cutest expression. She jumped from the couch and moved to cut off the chubby girl still latched on my arm. Chubs got the clue and went back outside.

"Oh, sexy man!" she said.

She took her place on my arm and smiled excitedly. I wondered how long she had worked here. Getting a good look at her face, she was at least 25 and I suspected she'd had some babies. She still had a very cute face with small lips and a little nose. Her black hair was pulled back into a braided ponytail.

"Sir, you want VIP room? It has shower," again asked the lady.

"VIP room, gooooood," exclaimed the massage girl.

"What are you going to do in the VIP room?" I asked her.

Blank look.

"Sorry, English no good."

The lady interjected, "You like the VIP room, only 500 baht. I do you discount, 400."

126

The little girl was now hanging off my arm with the cutest puppy dog face and feistily tugging on me as if to say, "Do the VIP room." Normally, at the very least I'd want to see what the actual options were, but I gave in. I just couldn't help it. I guess 400 baht for a one-hour massage in Thailand was my new maximum. I comforted myself that it was still a fraction of the cost of an hour massage in America.

She led me down a hallway to a room which shut completely with a sliding door Japanese style. Though it didn't compare to a high-end spa, it was clean with a portrait of a geisha and flowers in two corners. In the other corner was a small shower which she hurried to and turned on. I guess I was getting a shower. This girl seemed smart, at least a hell of a lot smarter than my first masseuse of the trip, didn't need this shower as much this time though.

She turned back to me and grabbed my belt and began undoing it.

"Ohh, sexy man!" she said. I wondered if she knew any other phrases.

"What's your name?" I asked.

"I'm Gib."

"I'm Nathan."

"Nanane?"

"Nay-than."

"Ne-tan?"

"Naaay-thaan."

"Nah-tahn?"

"Yes." *Rolling my eyes.*

"Oh, sexy man!"

After she removed my pants and my hardening dick sprung into view, she blushed and then started lifting my shirt. I helped her out until I was finally standing naked before her.

"Oh, sexy man!"

If you say so.

For the next five minutes, I stood in the shower while she soaped me down. She acted as if she'd never seen a naked white man before. I wish I had been able to communicate with her better.

She giggled when my dick stiffened as she lathered up my balls, then giggled again as she stroked it and it stiffened even more. As she soaped down my chest, there was a constant smile on her face. She looked as if soaping me down was the greatest thing she'd ever done in her life. By the time she finished with the shower, I wanted to throw her on the massage table and ravage her, but I still wasn't sure this was a sex house.

Next, she toweled me off meticulously with the ever-present giddiness. I was becoming giddy myself. I wasn't quite sure what was about to happen, but I was certain it would be wonderful. She made me feel like a superstar. If Brad Pitt went into a random massage parlor, this would likely be the reaction he received. *And my friends wonder why I go on sex excursions.*

When I exited the shower, I waited for her to jump on me, as I had forgotten that I was there for a massage. She walked to the other side of the massage table and said, "ok, face down please."

She was still grinning madly. I noticed she had pearly white teeth and they were straight and perfect. She was certain to have had braces in her life, which was confusing to me. If she didn't know any English, she was likely a new sex worker, where did she get the money? Anyway... shit, now I had to wait through a massage before I found out if I could bang her.

I plopped on the table facedown tucking my dick back. She immediately grabbed my ass and shook it a bit running her fingers over my balls.

"Wohh. You sexy man!"

I know honey.

I was even starting to believe it. I was a sexy, sexy man!

"Where are you from?" I asked as she began the oil massage.

"I'm from Ubon Thani."

That is North Isaan.

"How long have you been working here?"

"I don't understand."

"How long work?"

"Oh. Ummm. First time."

"First time?"

"First Farang."

"Oh, I see."

"Ehh?"

"Nothing. So… you like Farang?"

"Ugh!" she screamed in a positive way.

"No?"

"Ugh! Farang good."

"Ugh?"

"Ugh. Yes."

I get it, 'ugh' is like saying 'yeah.'

Things quieted down as she continued the massage. Certainly not the best massage I've ever received, not nearly as good as the 'legitimate' massage a few days ago, but then again, I was tense with anticipation of what would happen after the massage that I couldn't have cared less.

Only 15 minutes had passed until she commanded the flip. She still had not covered my butt with a towel and so my dick sprung into full view.

She wasted no time at all and grabbed my dick with her hand.

"Oh, big!" she laughed.

I laughed as well. If I was her first farang, maybe I actually did seem big to her.

"Handjob?" she asked.

Well, I guess that settled it whether this was a sex shop. I was disappointed, to say the least. The thought of leaving with only a handjob was terrifying.

I grabbed her little bubble butt. In response, she smiled even wider and arched her back to firm it up in my grasp as she continued teasing my dick.

I slid my hand up to pull her uniform out from her shorts to get a feel of her skin. Then, I ran my fingers under the back of her shorts to the top of her ass crack.

"You want take off?" she asked.

"Uh huh." *Obviously.*

"Mmmm, smoke?" she asked.

"Uh huh."

"Mmmmm," her face seemed lost in thought.

"One thousand, one hundred?" she asked. It seemed she was more asking if she got the words right than if the price was ok.

"One thousand, one hundred?" I repeated confused.

"Smoke, take off, one thousand, one hundred."

Somehow, I didn't think the price she was trying to tell me was 1100 baht, but I would deal with that later. At that moment, I became very impatient to have my dick in her mouth.

"Ok."

This seemed to please her, and her face showed no emotion other than pure delight as she took off her shirt and repositioned her ass closer to my face and leaned down to take my dick in her mouth.

She went to town on me with such enthusiasm that I momentarily missed the fact that only her shirt came off. She wasn't a particularly good head giver but the speed at which she was bobbing up and down was enough. She was excited to be servicing me.

Instead of attempting a conversation of "why didn't you take all your clothes off?" I simply reached my hand down the back of her shorts to feel her soft round little ass. She had a sexy ass for such a little girl. Each cheek was plump and created a tight fit as I pushed a finger down her ass crack.

She arched her back more in response and spread her legs slightly to loosen the clinch in her ass as she massaged my belly with one hand and rubbed my balls with the other, all the while madly slurping on my dick. I could feel saliva dripping down the sides of my crotch.

I managed to get a finger to the edge of her pussy where I could feel some hair. She was unshaven. I backed off a bit and instead kept pushing my finger between her ass cheeks eventually grazing her little asshole. She flinched a little, so I didn't push it any further.

After a couple of minutes, I was ready to erupt. I let the orgasm build trying not to call any attention to it, as I wanted to see her reaction as my cum entered her mouth. The only change in my demeanor was grabbing the far ass cheek and pulling it into the table to reduce her ability to jump away. Then, through willpower, I kept my hips still until the first squirt entered her mouth.

She gagged and lifted her head immediately. *Ahhhh! No fun!*

She then grabbed my dick with both hands and tugged until I was sensitive.

"Thank you!" she exclaimed when I handed her exactly 1100 baht.

I think she was trying to say 1000 baht and the extra 100 she thought was a tip. I was getting dressed as she stood next to the massage table in her jean shorts and bra smiling at me as if I was a movie star.

Recognize the girls who want more than money and be ready to let them down hard if necessary.

Many of the girls in Southeast Asia put foreigners on a pedestal. I like to think we get knocked down a peg or two as they begin to meet us and find out how many douchebags there are among us. This girl had not gotten a negative experience yet. I suspected she'd had a kid or two and was recently made single and decided that a foreigner would fix everything in her life. So, she got on the bus and came to Pattaya, but for a week or two, she had yet to meet one that fit her idea of a knight in shining armor. Until me, being sober (today), clean shaven, and white skinned.

"Outcall?" I asked her.

I desperately wanted to fuck this girl and it seemed she returned the desire, it was just a matter communicating it to her.

She gave me a blank look. I guess 'outcall' had not been taught to her yet.

"What time do you get off?"

Blank look.

"Off work?"

"Oh!" her face brightened up. "um. Six."

"Go with me?" I asked as slow as possible.

"Oh! You want boom me?" she asked showing me those pearly whites.

"Yes! You want?"

"Ugh!"

There was no mention of money whatsoever and I left the parlor that afternoon with a smiling happy girl expecting me to come back and pick her up. I've met girls on sex trips that seemed overly excited about getting to know me, far beyond the income they would generate from my company. I knew that's what I was getting into with Gib. In fact, if I had it to do over, I would have stood her up. I was on a sex trip, not a spoil-a-girlfriend trip or a bride-hunting mission. Recognize the girls who want more than money and be ready to let them down hard if necessary.

I knew from the moment I agreed to pick her up after work that she wouldn't just leave my condo after the deed was done, I'd have to throw her out, but her enthusiasm made me want to fuck her. I knew she would be great in bed, though I really had no idea.

I spent the afternoon drinking with Ben until I was halfway to blackout. When I'm drunk, I tend to not make the best decisions, in life, in relationships, and in dealing with sex workers. During that afternoon, I built up Gib in my mind to be a special girl and I had to show her a good time. She was no longer just a fuck.

Ben was no help when I asked him for a nice restaurant to take her to.

"Fuck, mate, just go to Central." As if I couldn't think of that.

So, I poured through google until I found a restaurant that seemed convenient from Soi Buakhao that had good reviews. It was on the intersection of Central Rd and Soi Buakhao so we could jump on a songthaew and be there in a flash. It was totally random, the kind of shit you think up when you are drunk, as if a new massage girl right off the bus would give two fucks about where I took her to eat, could have taken her to the food court across the street.

At 6, I bumbled down the row of beer bars, passing by all the available pussy calling out to me, on my way to engage in what I thought would be a meaningful relationship. She was waiting outside and had changed out of her massage uniform. She was still wearing the small jean shorts that showed off her cute little ass but was now wearing a cheap plain black loose shirt matching the color of her hair. When she saw me, she bounced with joy and her face brightened up with her pearly white smile and she strode away from her friends without even saying goodbye. In my inebriated state, my heart melted. Gib was not a supermodel, and not more beautiful than the girls I'd been with so far on the trip, but she was charming, and she seemed to be infatuated with me.

So, on this trip, I'd had my dick sucked in the hallway by a crazy underage girl. I'd shoved my dick down the throat of a nympho whore. I fucked a girl while she was getting her ass plowed. So far, it was a crazy sex trip, but it was really moments like this with Gib that I travel to Asia for -- to feel desired by a beautiful girl many years younger than me.

The big problem with Gib was communication, though. She had learned enough English to manage business in the massage parlor (barely) but having any kind of conversation was nearly impossible. Even the explaining of my desire to get in a songthaew in the direction of Central Road had to be done with charades. The whole time, she continued staring at me with that smile of admiration.

When we finally sat down at Leng Kee Restaurant, it felt awkward. I'd certainly paid for sex with girls that spoke no English but to take one on a date was uncommon for me, at least with the level of English Gib had.

"Beer?"

Blank look.

"Drink?"

A nod of the head and big smile.

"What drink?"

"Mmmm… Coke"

"No, drink!"

Blank look.

Once I finally get my beer….

Point to beer. "Drink!"

Shake of the head. "Don't like."

"No drink alcohol?"

"No."

That's right, Gib had never had alcohol and was not about to start on my account. While I'd begun to spend most of my trip drunk or hungover, Gib reminded me that I don't prefer that state. She was good for me, and again, my heart melted. This was the girl that I needed to get myself back together. She was everything I was looking for.

Leng Kee Restaurant had the best Thai food so far on my trip. Gib ordered some disgusting fish and rice combination that she managed after a lengthy conversation with the waitress. After the food arrived, it didn't seem to be what she was looking for. That's the problem of taking poor girls to a nice restaurant, as they may not even appreciate it. They are used to simple food.

I ordered chicken green curry and papaya salad and it was so amazingly delicious compared to the slop I had eaten with Ben in the Soi Buakhao food court. At over 5x the cost, it better be.

For most of the meal, I tried to ask questions of Gib through a series of google translate and showing pictures. I managed that she'd had two kids with two different Thai men who promptly dumped her after each was born. It was the typical story of "oh shit, I got pregnant by an asshole, and now I need to fend for myself. Better go fuck foreigners." Though, having sex was not her preference. Blowjobs, ok.

For the trip back to the condo, we took another songthaew in the opposite direction on Soi Buakhao. There were no other foreigners in the songthaew, it was full of Thais and finally, Gib could come alive in conversation, which of course seemed entirely about me.

It's a common occurrence when traveling, unfortunately, and I've become accustomed to either ignoring it or sitting with a big smile and assume they are saying flattering things. With Gib, I'm sure it was flattering, she didn't yet have a reason not to be. I suspect the ugly Thai lady on the other side was versing her in Farang bride lessons.

After exiting the songthaew on Soi Lengkee to make the short walk to my condo, she grabbed my hand and locked fingers. Though Gib had the fire of a young girl in a relationship, she also seemed to have the maturity of a girl who'd been around the block. She wasn't new to being with a man, but it was special for her this time, though I had not yet noticed that. At the time, I was simply drunk and ready to get my dick in her.

In the elevator, I got my first kiss. Finally alone together since the VIP room, she wasted no time in approaching me. She wrapped her arms around me and laid her head on my collar bone. With her size, that was as far up as she could reach. She rubbed my back feeling what muscles I had back there I guess.

"Sexy man," she sighed.

Then, she looked up at me and lifted herself on her tiptoes reaching for my lips. I leaned down and stuck my tongue in her mouth for the sloppiest kiss I could manage.

"Ahh, beer!" she laughed.

Well, at least she was a quick study in English.

When the door opened to my floor, she did not want to let me go and I stumbled out of the elevator tripping and dragging a hysterical Gib who was acting even more intoxicated than I was. In between butt grabs and crotch grabs, we made our way slowly and loudly down the hall toward my condo. I really should have had more respect for my neighbors, if not for their sake, but for mine as it seemed to always get me into trouble, though I had no idea at the time how this particular incident would affect me.

137

Approaching Ben's door, I should have expected it when he poked his head out.

"Hey, mate, thought I heard you."

"Sup," was about all I mustered.

"Hey, girly!" he said insisting on becoming part of our little party.

"Hello, sir!"

We continued stammering down the hall past the imposing Ben standing in his doorway with his gym shorts and wife-beater. I could see in his face he had continued the drinking while I was at dinner.

"Woo wee!" he yelled as we passed. "Look at that little ass!"

Some moments in life are just a bit of a surprise when they happen, but over time become emotionally staining. This was one of those moments for me. Gib shouldn't have been anyone special to either of us -- just another sex worker in Pattaya. So, when Ben knelt and planted both his hands on Gib's bubble butt and shook it as she hung off me, it should have had little effect on me. In fact, he probably thought we were going to share every girl from now on.

Gib instantly whirled around to the other side of me, her excitement vanishing and replaced by a stare of confrontation, ready to jump again at any further groping.

"Oh Jesus, Ben. She's not a bargirl," I said to him.

"What? Ha ha ha," Ben's booming laugh echoed through the hall. "No anal creampie?

"Send her over to me after you are through anyway," he stated seriously, as if it was an expectation, and disappeared back into his condo, one of the few times I was happy Gib couldn't understand English.

Not this time, you fucking pig of a human being.

Still a little bewildered when I got her through the door to my condo, I expected Ben to have put a serious damper on our night. Even a bargirl, I'd expect to be a little put off by the event, even though they get groped throughout the night in their jobs, they still expect to be treated with a little respect when in the hallway of a condo, for example. For a new massage girl, it could have been traumatizing.

Fortunately, Gib was not the kind of girl to let a nasty man ruin her special night. She stood straight up in the condo and put her hands on her hips and smiled.

"Asshole!"

"Yes."

She laughed as she looked around the condo.

"Oh very nice!"

I learned then that even with the unsolicited ass groping, this night was many times better than her typical night. A nice guy, a nice dinner, and now possibly the best residence she'd ever set foot in. I sat down on the couch to enjoy her reaction.

"Drink?" I asked her.

"No want. Want you."

She lunged at me with a passion I'd yet to experience from a girl in Thailand, attacking me like a drunk girl at a college party with the quarterback. Her smooth Thai legs squeezed me at the hips and her ass jutted out in her jean shorts as she lodged her tongue in my mouth and smooched my ears and neck.

I grabbed her best feature by running my hands under the back of her shorts all the way to her hairy bush again. This time, when I ran my finger over her asshole, she didn't balk one bit, except by grinding her ass into my legs. I couldn't help but run my fingers from butt cheek to butt cheek feeling the canyon from her sexy mounds down to her tight puckered little ass. It was the soft mature ass of a mother, but sitting on the frame of a girl that would probably never gain weight.

She acted as if she could have straddled me on the couch for another hour or so, but after two minutes max, I was picking her up and carrying her into the bedroom.

"Wee, he he he he," she laughed.

Reaching the bed, I dropped her and she bounced off the bed erupting into more laughter. I stripped my clothes.

She stripped off her shirt and bra to reveal a smooth flat belly and small tits, practically just nipple, very typical of skinny Asians who've had babies. When she stripped off her shorts and panties and I finally got a view of her hairy bush, I was practically astonished. So, this is what us sex tourists had to put up with in the 60s I bet. *No pussy eating for you dear.*

There would be no condom for this, I didn't even need to consider grabbing one. Since I met her for dinner, she treated me like a man who she wanted as a boyfriend, not as a customer, and since I assumed her fucking experience in Pattaya was rather limited, why the hell would I put a condom on? Anyway, I don't believe she would have given me a chance to reach for one anyway.

As soon as her panties were off and she was on the bed naked, her little body draped over her knees, she grabbed my cock and pulled it forward as she leaned back. I toppled on her, both of us enjoying the time immensely. She never let go of my dick until it was inside of her. She was as hungry as I as was.

When the shaft of my dick fully penetrated her already wet pussy, she relaxed and moaned in satisfaction, as if she'd finally gotten her fix. I lifted up on my arms and pounded her, releasing the stress of having waited an entire day. *The horror*.

After a bit of pounding, she pulled me close to lock lips and bodies together. It felt passionate as if we were making love, my dick sending emotions throughout my body as it slid in and out of hers. My nut was building, and she could feel it.

As per usual, I planned on pulling out and cumming on her stomach, as I'm not really into the idea of knocking up a girl from a 3rd-world country who already has a couple of children, but she seemed to be resisting that plan. She had moved her hands down to my waist and seemed to be holding my body into hers. Was she actually doing that or was I just looking for the excuse?

As I began erupting, she wrapped both arms around my lower back and pulled her hips onto my dick as if she wanted every drop to empty as deep into her as possible, all the while sucking on my tongue erotically.

As I rolled off and held her in the aftermath, I wanted to launch right into a chastisement.

'Are you crazy? You should use condoms in Pattaya!' Something silly and hypocritical like that.

The logistics of communicating it to her exhausted me. I doubted she would even understand the word 'baby.' So, I let it go… and fucked her the same way a few more times that night, you know, just to confirm that she didn't care about using condoms or pulling out.

"No have."

It was an amazing night with Gib. I was satisfied the way a man is after spending the night having some of the best sex of his life with a hot sexy young girl that acts like he's a rock star, and who is totally into it. Gib wasn't exactly a nympho, but she loved fucking and acted affectionately and loving the whole night. It wasn't a pay-for-sex encounter, it was an encounter of mutual attraction. It would seem weird when I gave her money.

In the morning, after another session exactly like the ones of the previous night, I had begun the lame process of the condom talk. It would have bugged me otherwise, was she trying to get pregnant with me or did she have no control? That would explain why she'd already had two kids with different men. After several minutes of tedious google translate and charades with pictures, she finally understood the subject.

"No have?" I repeated.

"Mmhmm... Cannot," she said.

"What do you mean 'can not?'" I asked.

She patted her belly and said again, "Cannot."

My first reaction was one of disbelief, which should be any man's reaction. Believing that a young girl can no longer get pregnant even though you know she's had a couple of kids already would be stupid. She obviously just wanted me to continue cumming inside her, that's why she held me deep. This bitch wanted to have a farang baby!

She must have sensed my growing anger and distrust. She grabbed her purse and pulled out a round packet of pills half punched out.

"Cannot."

It was the perfect reaction from her. I knew I was dealing with an educated woman, one who didn't want to get pregnant and understood that men don't like pulling out. But then I had some thoughts, 'Is she still married? Is there a Thai husband in the picture? I shouldn't mess around with a married Thai woman, that's a good way to get myself killed.'

'She could be playing me. Maybe she wants a farang baby, thinking it's a good way to extort me for money. Well, if that's the case, I'd have good reason to run away having seen a packet of used birth control.'

And... 'Just how much unprotected sex does she have? She seems new to dating farangs but it could all be a ploy. What if she goes bareback every day? What if I start burning?'

Of course, those thoughts quickly gave way to...

JACKPOT!

8

Koh Larn

In Thailand, there's not really a fine line between a pure sex trip and having a girlfriend while on a legitimate vacation. It's more of a solid glass wall. When you find yourself on the side of a traveler with a hot local girlfriend, you can see all the fun you'd be having on the other side of the wall, but it seems you'd have to smash the glass in order to get back to it.

It's for that reason, when I find myself on the wrong side of the glass wall, I tend to run a range of emotions from slight discomfort to full blown panic. My time in Thailand was limited, and being on that side of the wall meant not accomplishing the primary goal of the trip – having sex with multiple girls. It's always because I found something special in a girl, such as being able to cum inside her without a care in the world. It's easy enough though, to return to the other side, at least you'd think it would be, but when the breakup is made, someone always shatters, and if I'm lucky it'll just be her.

With Gib, I knew the eventual break-up would be even more profound, since she had not experienced it yet. I was her first farang, she was probably running the dream through her head of meeting a foreigner, traveling to America, and everything in her life being fixed, not to mention all the money she would make for her family. She may have even been texting her family already announcing the good fortune.

The tropical morning sun was peeking through the shades in our room at the charming family owned hotel I had spent the last few nights with Gib on the island of Koh Lanta. She lay asleep facing me, with a peaceful look on her face, a look of contentment like a puppy dog in the protective arms of its master.

I cared about her deeply. I'd spent ten incredible days with her in Thailand. There was no baggage, no bickering over payment, and despite, or perhaps because of, the language barrier which forced us to sit in silence most of the time, we were happy together at every silly moment, whether we were sitting on the beach or frolicking in bed. We did a ton of the latter.

We were flying back to Bangkok that day, and I had decided before we left that I would either end it with her upon returning to Pattaya, or spend the rest of my trip with her and accept that I wouldn't return to the sex tourist side of the glass. The shattering of the glass seemed unbearable to me, the thought of it pained me as if I would be destroying a human being in the process, and I wasn't sure which human would be more devastated.

But I'm getting ahead of myself, I wasn't even on Koh Lanta yet.

"Barfine one thousand."

How would you say 'no' to that face? Gib was a beautiful young lady in the face but also on the inside. It's just something you can tell about people, even without the communication. It's the expressions in their faces, their lack of confrontation, and their politeness even when it is unwarranted. Gib was all that, the kind of girl you'd bring home to mother and be proud of, so it was awkward to be speaking about barfines with her.

She was a daytime masseuse and had to be at work at noon, and the thought of us parting company so quickly after our first night seemed absurd to both of us. Fortunately, even masseuses in Pattaya can leave work on a barfine, that's not limited to bargirls. I eagerly agreed to pay the thousand baht barfine, and after a quick walk to her work, we headed to Pattaya beach outside of Central.

Don't travel halfway around the world just to save money on beer, have a purpose.

I was happy to be away from the slobbering egos of the British Bar and spending time with a wonderful girl. My thoughts and my body were relaxed, as I was doing exactly what I wanted to be doing without fear that I was missing out on anything. It's a pleasant state of mind for me, I only wish it would last longer. But hey, it's the alpha males that it lasts longer for, you know, the guys that get married at 18 and seem to be content with it their whole lives.

"Ugh!" Gib answered to my charades for choice of beach chairs. The way her face would light up with the 'ugh' any time she was getting her way was adorable.

Thailand can really do beaches. I've traveled to many tropical destinations from Mexico to Cambodia, and it seems no country does it as well as Thailand. As Thai beaches go, Pattaya is easily the worst, and even then, I'd take it over some Florida beach with its spaced-out beach chairs and lack of, or absurdly expensive, service.

In Thailand, there are always rows and rows of beach chairs, with umbrellas packed so tightly that the air under them gets cool from the permanent shade. In most sections of beach chairs, there is a full menu with cocktails, snacks, and entrees. Then there are the vendors, ranging from coolers of ice cream to local food to massages. Of course, the vendors may be hard to get used to for Westerners, but after some practice, the proper method of dismissing them becomes second nature. A simple wave of the hand to the floor and a shake of the head usually does it. When there is a persistent one, a scowl and turning away will do it, don't ever try to engage in argument or excuses. Once you have it down, you don't have to hide on one of the back rows of chairs where all the other Westerners are. We camped on the front row so we could watch all the beach goers pass by.

"Ooh," said Gib, pointing with enthusiasm at one of the vendors.

In one of the vendor's hands were several bags of small grey eggs with black dots that seemed to look dirty in some way. They were slightly larger than marbles and each bag had about 15. Quail eggs.

"Twenty baht," said the vendor.

"Ok, two," I replied, figuring since they were so cheap that I'd try a bag.

When I handed over the money, Gib became confused and began a rather lengthy conversation with the skinny middle-aged Thai man. They both would turn to me as if I was the subject, and I deduced it wasn't necessarily me they were discussing but all farangs. Gib was still new to dating a farang and had not yet learned about farang prices. I giggled proudly as I watched her learn a whole new concept. I was lucky I found her, before being taught that farangs are good for nothing more than ripping off, and I also wondered how cheap those eggs would be for Thais. 10 baht?

The eggs were just hard-boiled eggs, though extremely hard to deshell. I let Gib handle that, even though many of the pieces ended up in the sand. They seemed to go especially well with the lukewarm beer I enjoyed while leaned back in the chair watching her meticulously peel the pieces of shell from the egg, coating it in soy sauce squeezed from a little plastic bag, to feed to me while the parasails floated around in the ocean ahead of me. Ahh, Thailand.

I enjoyed it so much I wanted more of it, but I wanted it purer, not the grungy engine fumed beach of Pattaya. I'd read on forums about an island that was a quick day trip from Pattaya – Koh Larn.

"Tomorrow, go Koh Larn?" I asked her.

Blank look.

"Koh Larn!" I said and pointed across the water. Koh Larn is just visible from the beach.

Instant smile of joy. "Ugh!"

We spent the rest of the day lounging on the Pattaya beach drinking beer for me, tea for her, eating quail eggs and ice cream of which I enjoyed the quail eggs more due to the melted and refrozen state of most of the vendor ice cream, and making fun of the Westerners that walked down the beach.

"Oh, poompwee!" laughed Gib at a plump middle-aged white couple.

A little later we laughed at the grey-haired lady floating all by herself in the ocean on the wrong side of the swimming dividers. She seemed annoyed at the speedboat that pulled up beside her as if that was her spot and the boat was being rude. No, lady, you are in the wrong place. I wonder if it was arrogance that caused her to sit there, or if she was just nervous about being in a foreign country and didn't take the time to observe her surroundings. It's obvious there is a big swimming area and the rest of the beach is where the boats come in.

Most travelers come to Thailand without a clue. They heard it's a friendly place with beautiful beaches and cheap beer and jumped on a plane, but then they don't even get to know a single Thai person beyond the waiter that keeps them inebriated through the whole trip. Traveling alone often gives someone the opportunity to become immersed in another culture and it's a means for personal growth if nothing else. Don't travel halfway around the world just to save money on beer at the beach, have a purpose.

I wonder how many judgments were hurled back in my direction that afternoon – a middle-aged balding and boring Western man with a charismatic woman 25 years younger sitting on the beach in a foreign country taking advantage of their poverty completely self-absorbed and incapable of true love. My purpose was getting my dick wet, though I liked to pawn it off as being cultural.

"Oh my God, so poompwee!" screamed Gib at the appearance of a rather obese Western couple.

Well, at least I wasn't poompwee!

I awoke the next morning eager for our side trip to Koh Larn, though the evening before had taken an unexpected turn. Since Gib had a job, I had not yet thought that when I was ready to get rid of her it would be much of a problem.

I'd simply refuse to barfine her and then ignore her texts. *Easy.*

Don't allow a Thai girl to quit her job for you.

In the evening after the beach, we stopped by the massage parlor again to pay the barfine for the following two days as I planned to spend a night in Koh Larn so we could explore the island. There was a heated conversation between Gib and the old lady and I would later discover that she wanted 3,000 for the barfine even though the 3rd day was her regular day off. Gib and I assumed the barfine would be only 2,000 and then she wouldn't have to go to work for another three days. Thai logic didn't quite see it that way, three days off in a row to spend with a farang meant three barfines must be paid.

Instead of asking me for the 3,000 which I would have paid over the alternative, Gib simply quit. Somehow, I didn't think her plan was to look for another job when we returned from Koh Larn.

My relationship would have to be dealt with at some point I knew... or not dealt with which would mean spending the rest of my time in Thailand with her. Neither option appealed to me, there is no happy middle ground on that kind of deal. There is no compromise that allows me to fuck bargirls with Ben while she remains the same enthusiastic naïve girl with her first farang. I let those thoughts consume me for most of the night and the morning on the way to the ferry until I managed to let it go and enjoy my getaway from Pattaya.

The ferry was a large crowded boat with two levels of wooden chairs and plenty of life jackets. I marveled a little at all the people who donned a life jacket. It was as if I was transported back to America where safety was a big deal. Gib responsibly grabbed a pair to which I expressed an "I'm too macho to wear that."

She placed her hands on her hips, smiled, and then scrunched her mouth and widened her eyes as if I was going to get trouble. Uh oh, don't hurt me, you 80-pound soaking wet Thai angel. Perhaps she knew that the Thai officials were about to line up in front of the boat and announce their requirement of life jackets.

I either got the farang pass or more likely, they didn't truly care. I've never been forced to wear a life jacket or seat belt (or helmet until recently) in Southeast Asia. I stayed sat in my outside wooden chair a little way from them and acted oblivious, though in a small way, I hoped they'd single me out for a life jacket, just for the story I could tell Ben, "Mate, you think you could fit in one of their life jackets?"

Instead, the officials took a picture of the whole deck, then turned around and left me utterly disappointed. I guessed the picture was to prove to someone they put everyone in their life jackets, and I thought the next time I'd make it a point to stand up for their picture so a bare-chested farang would be clearly visible. Gib smiled and laughed at me as she removed her life jacket. It seemed like it would smother her before she could fall in the water anyway.

Unbeknownst to me at the time, there are two different ferries to Koh Larn, one that takes you to Tawaen Beach, the most popular of the island and one that goes to

Naban, the main village on the island. We ended up on a ferry to the village and not the beach which I would have preferred. My desire was to get a room on the beach.

After a 90-minute ferry ride, we were in Naban and in similar fashion to all my experiences on islands, looked for a motorcycle to rent, and found myself completely lost in language barriers, or there were no rentals there, I'm really not sure. After some frustration from standing in the middle of a few Thai faces, including Gib, looking at me like I'm a monkey flapping his arms, I pointed at what looked like a beach on a map of the island that one of the motorbike taxis handed to me.

Always look at the room before booking in Thailand.

"50 baht, you want hotel?" asked the motorbike taxi.

"Yes."

"Ok, I take care you," he said.

Well, he had a bit more English than Gib anyway.

After a short ride over the top of the island, a gorgeous white sand beach appeared. Gorgeous except that it already seemed busy, way busier than any of the beaches at Pattaya. The beach sat in a broad cove flanked by green rounded hills. Though not the majestic limestone of southern Thailand, it had its own appeal.

There were lodges and shops running the length of the beach and the driver took us to the first hotel. It was shit, and so was the next one. I wondered if he was getting a commission for these or if he was just clueless to a foreigner's taste. He didn't seem disappointed though when I told him to get lost and continued down the beach on foot.

Always look at the room before booking in Thailand, refunds are hard.

It wasn't long until I came to a modern resort with a well-staffed open-air restaurant that looked a class above the ones beside it. I believe the name was something original like "Tawaen Beach Resort." I asked to see the 2nd-floor beach view room priced at 2,500 baht, and though it was more of an ocean view room due to all the umbrellas in front of the resort, it was perfect.

We dropped our bags and headed out to the beach for a quick lunch. As we walked through the hotel, I noticed that none of the rooms were booked, we seemed to be the only guests, which was odd to me given the multitudes of people already on the beach.

The hotel had a section of beach chairs with the fully shaded umbrellas typical of Thailand beaches. One of the young Thai men that showed us around the hotel initially guided us to a couple of chairs in front informing us there was no charge since we were guests of the hotel. That knocked 200 baht off the rate at least.

"You want menu? We have full menu," he said.

Of course we did, and I'd eat green curry chicken and a papaya salad, while Gib nibbled on a smelly fish and rice plate that seemed to stink up the entire section of beach chairs. I passed on the alcohol as Gib wouldn't have a drink no matter how I pressed her, and I was fine with that. Instead, I had a frozen virgin Pina Colada and relaxed to people watch.

"Oh, very beautiful!" remarked Gib at a fair-skinned Asian couple walking by.

Our view seemed quite different from the beach in Pattaya. The overweight Westerners must not have been up for the ferry ride and instead only young fit Asian couples made the journey. I missed the *poompwee* couples of Pattaya. I felt superior there. On Tawaen Beach, I didn't even have the best-looking girlfriend, that title definitely went to the supermodel Japanese man and his runway model Japanese girlfriend that caused Gib to be momentarily lost in admiration. I bet he's got a small cock, was the only thought with which I could comfort myself.

After eating, we sat in the surf for a half-hour to let the food settle. Well, I say surf, it was more like wakes from all the speedboats transporting an infinite supply of Asian tourists to the beach. The sand between our hotel's umbrellas and the water was being filled in by Thai families and other tourists from around the world, including a good number of Indians, who didn't seem to smell at all worse than the other beachgoers, and in fact, they seemed more polite than the Thai family who usurped our little spot in the waves. Oh well, it was time to see the island, before the whole beach became an obstacle course. It frightened me what the beach would look like at night, and I hoped the hotel would be somewhat quiet.

It was 2 pm by the time we showered off the sea water, changed clothes, had a quickie, and then showered off the sex for good measure. When we were walking the same stretch from our hotel down to the road where the taxi-bike dropped us off, it didn't even seem like the same island. It was packed like Miami Beach on Memorial Day. The ferry boat was big, but it didn't seem as if the half-dozen or so trips that it made in the morning could have transported this many people. There must have been literally hundreds of speedboat runs made as well.

There were plenty of motorbikes for rent, fortunately. I found the obvious "anything you want to do with motorbikes" section of the beach. It was 300 baht for the motorbike rental until night and I didn't have to pay for gas. I paid the 300, took the helmets they made me take, buckled them to the back hand grip, and was off!

I'm not a motorcycle enthusiast by any stretch but to ride the motorbikes in Thailand, you hardly need more than experience on a bicycle. Some of the most memorable moments in my life were on a Southeast Asian island with a hot young girl when I was let loose on a motorbike. And let loose I did. I tore up that hill with a vengeance, eager to rid my world of the Asian crowds.

"Oh, slowly, slowly, honey!" screamed Gib.

Gib wrapped her tiny arms around me and squeezed tight. I loved it. I didn't slow down much, and she got used to it.

Koh Larn was a rural little island, a fact hard to notice if sitting under the umbrellas of Tawaen Beach. In just a couple minutes, we were back in Naben, the little village where our ferry docked earlier. The village was an ordinary Thai village with a large square and loads of idle people and various shacks acting as stores interspersed with modern resorts and convenience stores. I kept going through the village, my only plan being to keep riding.

The road curved out of the village and headed south on the island. It gained a little altitude and passed through a grassy field that afforded beautiful views. We stopped for a bit to look around and I spied the highest point on the island which contained a large Buddha statue just below it, which again is typical of Thailand, what good is a hill if there is not a religious monument on it? After following the road to the south, we'd head to the statue.

After a five-minute ride, the road ended at a lovely little beach. We parked for a short time to explore the beach. This is the kind of beach I'd be more into and I began to regret not finding a motorcycle before finding a room. The beach was sparsely populated, though still with the rows of beach chairs and umbrellas. There was a large restaurant but after looking did not see any actual rooms for rent. It seemed it was just a beach and even though was less populated than where we were staying was still busy for a beach with no rooms. It was then that I started to wonder where all those people were going to go at the end of the day.

We relaxed on "Monkey Beach" for an hour or so but as there was limited daylight left, had to get back on the bike to find the statue. I wanted to see the island from its highest point before night. After one set of bad directions and one set of good directions when I let Gib be in charge of getting us there, we finally found the road to the Buddha statue at an intersection nearly back at Tawaen Beach. The statue was just a statue, like all the other Buddha statues. We stopped for selfies and then continued up the hill.

In Pattaya, there is a Buddhist shrine and attraction similar to the one at Koh Larn, though grander. I assumed they existed all over Thailand. Led by the imposing Buddha statue visible to most of the island, the road winds into an area with various religious attractions and stores with the occasional monk. I believe the purpose of it is to stop in, buy essence, and then pray at one of the many shrines. The shrines range from a small gold icon to a large concrete effigy, or the Buddha statue itself. I drove on until the road dead-ended at a small hut with paths leading up two hills. I knew from other travels I was allowed to go anywhere that a door wasn't closed so I strode straight into the hut to look around.

Be honest with yourself and everyone you meet on your trip, you are a sex tourist.

"Good evening sir."

I've never seen a smile so pure and honest on anyone in Thailand. The tall slender Thai elder in a monk robe carrying a wooden water bucket turned to me with one of the most genuine expressions of welcome I've ever received in my life. There was a moment there that I wanted to give up all my wicked ways and convert to Buddhism in an attempt to have what he had. Enlightenment?

"Hello, I... uhh... want to go up there," I said pointing at a lookout.

"Oh very nice, that way," he said pointing to a path. "Where are you from?"

"America."

"How are you enjoying your trip?" he continued.

"It's so amazing! It's my first time here, I'm here on business in Pattaya." *What did I say?*

His English was fluent, possibly Western educated. It was a relief to be able to have a real conversation without the need to bust out Google translate, and I took advantage of it. I lied about my purpose in Thailand, explaining that I was there on business and how beautiful the country was. I explained what a wonderful girl Gib was and that I was considering marrying her even though she didn't speak any English.

And then... I panicked for a bit when he broke into Thai with Gib and she brightened up in pure delight. That's the problem with lying, even to persons you'll never see again, it always comes back to bite you. What was wrong with telling him I was there to buy pussy? Nothing. He would have respected me for telling the truth whereas, in my encounter with him, he probably thought of me as the worst sort of person. That is, if he judged at all, that's the intent of Enlightenment, to free yourself of judgments. Be honest with yourself and everyone you meet on your trip, you are a sex tourist. Besides, then I would have gotten to see the look on his face when I said, 'I'm here to fuck 19-year-olds. This one is a little old for me, don't you think? Should I get rid of her?'

But I couldn't help being jealous of the man as we made our way towards the lookout. For those fleeting moments in my life when I sunk my dick into a girl's mouth, I was content. I wondered if I could find contentment living my life on the top of a hill maintaining a shrine and helping others with their religious devotion. Bah... he must be profiting off the poverty on the island, I told myself, though I didn't really believe.

The lookout was an aging concrete structure with a standing Buddha statue and shrine in the center, a short climb up from the hut with magnificent views over the island and the surrounding ocean. Across the water in the failing light, I could make out Jomtien beach south of Pattaya and below us ran the length of Tawaen beach still seemingly packed with people, though I noticed most of the boats heading in the opposite direction.

I wrapped up Gib to enjoy the evening sun washing over the island. Was she the one to end all my scandalous ways? If every moment could be like that one, I'd give it an easy yes. Too bad life doesn't work that way. After several minutes we made our way down and I looked for the path to the higher point, which I deemed the highest on the island.

After making our way back through the hut and feeling the warmth of the tall monk's incredible smile, we found the path by way of a big red arrow on a sign that read Buddha's Footpath – 250 steps. Well, that would be the perfect way to end the day, climb a mountain.

It was slow going in my flip-flops on the tiny concrete steps, laughing with Gib as she'd take a quick few steps and then wait for me. In America, these steps would likely be remade the first time someone tripped and skinned their knees. I thoroughly enjoyed the climb now that the day was cooling off and the sky in the west was developing a brilliant orange color.

On the top of the hill stood a well-maintained concrete hut protecting a gold Buddhist shrine with urn for burning essence. These shrines are present all over Thailand, there is even one outside the condo where I stayed. Gib would often put her hands together in front of her chest when we passed. The shrine on this hill seemed a cast above most with a mural of a goddess, and a well-crafted gold Buddha legs-crossed on top of the shrine.

"Ohh, come," said Gib.

She sat down on her knees and motioned for me to sit across from her. Then she lit an essence and held it in her hands in front of her mouth in a praying stance.

"You," she said handing me essence.

I realized she intended to have me pray with her. I'm not a religious person but sitting down with a beautiful girl to have a spiritual moment was right up my alley at the time. In fact, the whole day was a freeing experience, I felt I was on my way to Enlightenment already.

She closed her eyes, whispered something in Thai, and then nodded her head in prayer.

"You, go. Anything," she said.

I understood that I could pray for anything. I closed my lids until I had a slit of vision which all I could see was Gib's skinny knees. It was obvious what I would pray for. I began to think about taking her right there in front of the shrine. Would she allow me to? I planned my assault. After we were done, I'd reach over for a hug and rub her back lovingly and then as we parted, I'd kiss her and then act as if the kiss set a fire in me. I pictured myself laying her on her back in front of the Buddha, taking her shorts off, and dropping my semen inside of her right there.

It didn't take long to plan, far less than the novel of a prayer she must have made. I laid my essence on the small wooden table and sat there staring longingly at her until she finally opened her eyes.

She looked around and immediately busted up laughing. "Noo!" she said.

She grabbed the essence and placed it in the urn with the other sticks of essence. *Duh!*

Laughter leads to sex, I thought, and considered myself fortunate she didn't exit her prayer to some kind of melancholy. I leaned in for the kiss.

She responded with an affectionate kiss and smiled.

I leaned in for a bigger kiss and moved my body closer so I could grab her butt and quickly progress the mood. She didn't seem to be resisting. Did I score a jackpot with this girl or what? She even seemed to be into it more than me, and our embrace quickly turned sexual.

I reached my hand down to the button on her shorts to communicate my desire and see her reaction. Not the slightest flinch. When I used both my hands to undo them, she looked at me and laughed in amusement. She knew I was wanting some naughty sex. When I moved my hands to the sides of her shorts, she stood up and walked to the door of the shrine to look in the direction of the stairs. Probably a good call, it might ruin some skinny monk's day to find a farang banging some young girl at the foot of his Buddha shrine.

"Fast, fast," ordered Gib as she returned to me and slid off her shorts.

I was astonished, I didn't think she'd let me get anywhere, much less play an active role. I thought "fast, fast" was probably a good idea as I relieved my cock of the zipper and collapsed on top of her sliding myself inside and putting my tongue in her mouth.

As I pounded her on the floor of the shrine watching the smile on her face get bigger and bigger, I wondered what her prayer was. Maybe it simply wasn't a big deal for Thais to bump-uglies on the floor of a holy place, but when she turned her head in the direction of Buddha, it gave me a different thought. Perhaps her prayer was to start a family with me and my immediate desire to take her then and there was some kind of confirmation of her wish. The thought heightened my experience.

Gib arched her back to keep the cushioned part of her butt on the hard concrete as I hastened to bring myself to orgasm until we finally moaned in unison in the presence of the great Buddha as I emptied inside her.

"Woo, very fast," she exclaimed as she pulled her shorts on. I wondered if it was better to let my semen drain in her shorts rather than the floor of the shrine. I giggled at the latter thought and let her handle it. And yes, I was very fast, probably cumming in 30 seconds, which was a good thing as we could hear shouts from a group of Thais heading up the stairs.

Gib was still beaming with happiness when the group of kids appeared. She exchanged pleasantries in Thai and we began down the stairs. The sun was setting on the dark orange horizon over the ocean and I found myself famished from all the walking and sex, and small dangerous stairs be damned, I was ready to find some food and started hopping down the stairs as best I could.

"No, Farang!" screamed Gib.

"Farang, Ting-Tong!" she added with an eruption of laughter from the kids behind her.

"What is Ting-Tong?"

Laughter. "You! Ting-Tong!"

She was calling me a Ding-dong[14]! It's ok, I probably looked like a ding-dong. I could have looked like a bloodied-up ding-dong if I kept trying to hop down the stairs like a 16-year-old. After some time, we were finally on the bike and heading away from the big Buddha.

In no hurry to brave the crowds of Tawaen Beach, I turned right and headed for Naben. When I passed by the town square earlier, I saw a collection of food stalls and thought that would be a nice experience. It would certainly

---

[14] Ting-tong comes from an adaptation of ding-dong though Thais use it more as an exclamation of "crazy" or "loco," without the connotation of "silly" where Westerners may use ding-dong.

make Gib more comfortable being around all Thais instead of an assortment of Asian tourists.

I was pleasantly surprised at the assortment of food and beverage. It ranged from fresh seafood to burgers to espresso. Yep, I just had to try the espresso from the little coffee stall that was tastefully decorated like a boutique coffee shop, while I ate papaya salad and chicken on a stick. I exclaimed to the coffee shop owner, a 50-year-old Thai lady that her coffee was the best thing I'd had yet on the island. That may have been an exaggeration, though it was certainly the strongest thing I'd had on the island, and it was nice to have a little buzz.

Gib had a simple and charming way about her, joking with all the vendors as we perused the food on the display, most of whom didn't speak more English than her. I wondered if they believed us to be a dating couple or if they assumed every Westerner with a Thai lady was a sex tourist. It was probably the latter. While Koh Larn was thousands of miles away from Pattaya in terms of culture, it was still a mere one-hour ferry ride in travel time. Yet, the interactions in the homey Thai village of Naben gave me that familiar feeling of being in a relationship, and I couldn't help but feel like that was not what I was in Thailand for.

Finally, it was time to head back to Tawaen Beach as I was expected to have had the motorbike back by now. When I pulled into the beach, I was astonished at how deserted it was. As I drove past the folded-up beach umbrellas, I could see clear to the water and the beach was lacking a single sole. The shops were closed with only a few lights on at some of the resorts, including mine. I knew I was at the right beach though and realized that all those beachgoers brought in during the day were taken back to

Pattaya in the evening, back to their guesthouses where they could partake in the Pattaya nightlife. I became giddy in what looked like a beach we'd have all to ourselves.

It was a calm night with a half-moon hanging low above the hills behind the beach. The ocean caressed the beach with a soft tranquil rhythm. I dropped the bike off at the resort and walked directly out to the beach with Gib hanging under my arm. When I reached the water, I stood in the peacefulness and held Gib on my chest. We were the only couple standing on that dark beach with the only light shining from two resorts with dim lights and the moon in the sky behind them.

"Weeeeee! He he he he," giggled Gib as she broke my grasp and ran down the beach in the water.

Ah well, what the hell, I thought as I took off after her, a nearly 50-year-old man chasing a mid-20s energetic girl down the beach. I was in heaven. She looked back at me as I gained on her splashing through the water like children.

Just as I had my hands on her, she darted sideways away from the water leaving me unbalanced in my attempted change of direction and *splat* right into the water. I cracked up and Gib was rolling in the aisles. *Oh yea, you laughing at me?*

Regaining my feet, I tested just how quick she really was as she was going into the water as well if I had anything to say about it. Having considerably longer legs and in decent physical shape at that time in my life allowed me to gain on her so long as she was going in a straight line, but she learned quickly that I had no hope of staying with her if she zigzagged around the beach… and that's how it went for about five minutes until finally, I hunched over in exhaustion looking at Gib standing upright giggling with hysteria, triumphant in our little game of catch me if you can.

Then we sipped virgin Pina Coladas at our resort until it was time to retire for the night. It was an exhausting day that I spent with a beautiful person, and is an experience I haven't had back home in the states for decades. Days like that made it all worth it, but there was still that uneasy feeling in me, a dishonesty I was playing on Gib and I could not find a sufficient way to deal with it considering the lack of communication.

9

Koh Lanta

"Ah, come on, mate. You gotta let me hit that."

The day after our magical trip to Koh Larn, I found myself downing more beer at the British Bar after numerous texts from Ben. It's as if I had a farang stalker. Gib and Porn had taken an immediate liking to each other and commandeered the lone pool table, turning the heads of the half-dozen Brits at the bar with every adorable giggle.

"Ben, haven't you ever met a girl here you didn't treat like a whore?" I asked.

"Nah, mate, they are all whores."

"This one is not for sharing."

"So, what? You gonna marry her? Bring her home and make a proper woman out of her?"

Though Ben was getting on my nerves with every word he uttered about wanting to fuck Gib, I could not deny the point he was making. On my sex trips, I often consider the black and white scenario of treating them like either whores or wives and there being no middle ground. It makes sense as if the relationship is not going to be permanent, there shouldn't exist any sort of ownership in either direction. I wasn't going to marry Gib, but I wasn't going to share her with anyone while she was with me either. I was sitting squarely in that grey area.

"Thousands of girls in Pattaya like her, man," I said.

"True, mate, but none of them have an ass like that," he said.

"So, if I find you one with an ass like that, you'll give up on her?"

Ben laughed. "Probably not, mate, not if you keep bringing her around me, but feel free to find me a little girl with that kind of bubble butt. Damn!"

Soon, I became distracted from our conversation when Farang Bob interrupted the girls' pool game with his usual drunken antics. The big man was chasing them around the table flailing his arms about in an attempt to be charming but failing due to his cocky but stressed demeanor. The girls were clearly annoyed.

He seemed annoyed that they were annoyed. I'm sure in his mind, they existed in the bar for his amusement and by not spoiling him with attention were breaking the rules of Pattaya. Porn was used to dealing with him though and confidently stood up to him while Gib hid behind her not sure what to make of the attack.

"I'll sit with you if you let us finish our game!" yelled Porn.

By now the whole bar was watching the commotion.

"Ah come on, honey, I need you. Let's go somewhere!" Farang Bob said and pushed in for an unwelcome hug.

"No no no!" yelled Porn while backing away. "Go! Sit down!"

With that, the imposing man backed away in defeat and sat opposite us at the bar with a scowl on his face after receiving another beer.

"Where did you find that bitch?" he asked, turning his gaze to me.

"Yea man, she's the problem, she's why Porn won't fuck you, right," I answered.

"You need your fucking teeth knocked out, don't you?" Ben taunted.

In stature, Ben and Farang Bob were roughly equal, though Ben had not let his body go and was 15 years younger, so I was sure Ben would win that brawl. Farang Bob seemed to know it too and retreated to sulking in his beer, while the Brits on our side of the bar laughed and the Brits on his side of the bar dropped their heads and smirked where he couldn't see.

Meanwhile, the girls were finishing their game of pool and had become even more animated in their conversation and giggles. Porn was surely talking about the ridiculousness of Western men, explaining how she had milked Farang Bob for a couple of hundred Baht every day for a month just by sitting in his lap, and how he kept coming to the bar in hopes he could take her to bed, which would never happen. I knew the whole experience that Porn lived every day was a new idea to Gib, and I hoped she never decided to live it herself. I'm not sure why, but handjobs and the occasional head at a massage parlor seems like a better choice than dealing with drunken pricks – or maybe I was simply getting jealous and protective of my new girlfriend.

The mood at the bar cooled down for a while with no one wanting to agitate Ben and Bob while the girls kept up their playful afternoon with Porn seeming to procrastinate in her promised visit to Farang Bob's lap.

It worked out nicely for me as I was busy planning my next getaway from Pattaya with Gib. A coworker had recently moved to Koh Lanta, an island in southern Thailand, with his American wife to live the dream while working remotely. Koh Lanta is a popular tourist destination for divers, beach lovers, and those who want to get away from the overcrowded islands like Phuket and Koh Samui but don't want to fully give up on amenities. According to my friend, it also has a strong infrastructure for the local population with reliable high-speed Internet.

I booked a flight from Bangkok on Air Asia to Krabi and checked out the hotels and transportation to the island. There seemed to be numerous van companies that ran from the airport. I used Agoda to browse a few hotels on Koh Lanta but per my usual M.O. would decide on the hotel after we arrived. Though only back from Koh Larn for a day, the atmosphere of the bar made me long to be out of Pattaya again.

Finally, Porn and Gib finished their game and they both came to sit with Ben and me, causing the scowl on Farang Bob's face to deepen.

"Are you ready to go on another trip?" I asked Gib.

Blank look.

"Tell her I have to go to Koh Lanta tomorrow to visit a friend and I want her to come with me," I said to Porn for the translation.

I could see the surprise and jealousy in Porn's eyes as she relayed my message to Gib. I felt like the most desirable man in the bar. I knew Porn would rather be in Gib's place, about to go on a vacation to a beautiful island, instead of spending her day drinking watered down cocktails and being groped in the laps of sloppy farangs. I wanted to be temporarily single just to see if she'd barfine with me, even though the jealous reaction would never have happened if I were single.

"Proper woman already," Ben snickered.

"Yes! She's very lucky!" Porn yelled.

169

Finally, Farang Bob's lack of attention was too much, and he yelled across the bar. "Hey, you said you'd come here!"

Porn's face dropped as she peered at him out of the corner of her eye.

"Ben, buy me drink?" she asked.

"Of course, dear," he answered and smirked in Farang Bob's direction.

As Porn hopped on the bar stool next to Ben, we all watched Farang Bob's face waiting for some ridiculous reaction, but he only stewed for a few seconds and then jumped from the bar and strode down the street.

"Hey, you pay!" screamed the older Thai lady behind the bar.

The whole bar laughed.

When visiting an island in Thailand, opt for a scooter rental sooner rather than later.

Morning broke and we were up at the crack of dawn to make the trip into Bangkok. The flight left early from Don Muang Airport which is further away from Pattaya than the main airport. Instead of mess with public transportation through Bangkok which would have meant a bus, two trains, and another bus, I grabbed a taxi for the whole trip to the airport. It ran me 2000 baht, which seemed expensive considering the fare to the main airport was only 1200 baht. I give drivers a break on it though, as I was once a cab driver. A three-hour drive in the states would run

$200 easy, and the fare to Don Muang was barely $60. Considering how I struggled as a cab driver in the states, I can't imagine the struggle of the Thai cab drivers. Cars and gasoline cost roughly the same no matter where you are in the world.

Gib was practically bouncing in her seat for the whole flight, it being her first time on an airplane. She showed no trepidation at all as the plane lifted over Bangkok, her face glued to the window.

The Krabi airport seemed more westernized than any place I'd been so far in Thailand, maybe with the intent of catering to the multitudes of tourists there to island hop. While most Westerners I met in Pattaya and Bangkok were middle-aged men like me, Krabi was full of young couples and groups of college students. Someone told them Thailand was the place to go and that's what they did.

The van companies were aggressively hawking their services at the exit of the airport and if I had it to do over again, I would have walked by them and looked for a scooter to rent. Though Koh Lanta was only a 1-2 hour drive, the van we were stuffed in doubled that time by stopping in Krabi to drop off and change vans. I was thoroughly annoyed. When visiting an island in Thailand, opt for a scooter rental sooner rather than later.

The drive was pleasant, however, with some novice Western travelers to converse with and I finally got a view of some of Thailand's famous limestone cliffs, though nothing like the pictures I'd seen of islands such as Koh Phi Phi and Phuket.

We crossed a ferry to Koh Lanta. Koh Lanta itself didn't seem to have any cliffs of its own. It was more like Koh Larn, though much larger. It had green rolling hills and was well developed. The island is shaped like a hand-held shower head facing east with the most popular beaches running the long west shore and a pleasant fishing and tourist city named Sala Dan sitting near the northwestern point. The island has a majority Muslim population with women in burkas a common sight, which I thought was a shame as Thai women are simply too beautiful to be covered up.

I told the driver to let us off at the first motorcycle rental shop, but as we passed through the main city of Sala Dan, I noticed numerous shops. I figured he was taking us to one he got a kick-back from so I again told him to stop at the next one. He said "ok."

Then another motorcycle shop passed and by now we seemed to be heading out of the main city, and I began to get frustrated.

"Hey! Are you going to stop?" I yelled at him.

The kids in the van opened their eyes in terror. I'm sure they were used to simply being at the whim of whatever a 3rd world driver wanted to do with them.

"Yes, I stop next one."

I wasn't convinced though and I climbed over the row of kids in front of me and lodged myself between the side door and the front row to watch for the next shop and once I spotted one on the right, I pointed across the passenger side and commanded to him, "Stop, right there!"

"Yes, ok, no problem," he answered, but the van wasn't slowing down.

As it became obvious he was going to pass by that shop too, I leaned across the kids, who were now frozen in shock, and grabbed the driver's shoulder. "STOP!" I yelled so loud it startled him, and the van lurched in a hard brake causing me fall in the small space between the front seat and the front passenger door.

"Goddammit!" I yelled.

One kid in the back laughed but the rest of the van was dead quiet, I guess afraid I was going to do something nuts. I calmed down though knowing I'd gotten the dumbass to drop us off. I pulled out our bags and we were finally standing on the road in Koh Lanta.

I usually don't lose my cool with Thais like that as 9 times out of 10 it is a matter of miscommunication. The driver probably thought he heard me say the name of some hotel as none of the normal young Westerners ask to be dropped off at a motorcycle shop having already made their reservations online and we were going to end up on the other side of the island with a confused look on his face. Regardless, it's important to take control and not let someone waste your time or take advantage of you.

Sex tourists aren't supposed to fall in love.

On a scooter at the price of 200 baht per day, we had lunch at a roadside Thai shop and then I got to the task of finding a hotel. Since we were already in the area, I stopped by some hotels on the appropriately named Long Beach on the west of the island. The hotels were widely dispersed along the road and I had trouble finding most of them.

The hotels were either too expensive for my taste or too basic, and we kept moving up the road until reaching Sala Dan. Sala Dan was more condensed than Long Beach and I was thankful I didn't find a hotel yet as I'd much rather be there so we could browse the shops and restaurants on foot. The multitudes of Western tourists, most of them in their early 20s, was a bit of a shock to me. How could a convenient island like Koh Larn be 90% Asian tourists and this far out-of-the-way island be 90% Western tourists? It must have something to do with marketing.

I drove to the end of the road toward what I deemed the corner of the island until I came to a beautiful little grassy knoll with a few hotels lining it. I parked the bike and knew this was the spot for me. In the middle of the grass there was a large cabana with an open-air Thai massage and beyond that was a wide sweeping beach. The sun was about an hour away from setting beyond a small rocky island with two palm trees that lined a broad sandy reef. It must have been low tide and one could walk for a good half mile beyond the shore. It was a stunning sight and I was gaining respect for the island.

I chose a 3-story hotel with large balconies overlooking the knoll and facing the beach, named Aloha Lanta Resort. Inside, it was a basic and aged building but well-kept and clean. It was run by a friendly Thai family with a hardworking father who spoke little English and handled all the maintenance while his teenage son who spoke near-perfect English handled all the customer service. There was no sign of the mother while I stayed.

At the quoted rate of 1500 baht per night, the room would have needed to be a real shitpit for me to not be happy so I suspended my normal rule of seeing the room first and booked it, and found the room to be a great value with a modern bed and furnishings, though the real treat was the balcony that I saw from outside. It would be the perfect stay for a few nights.

As the sun continued its slow plunge into the sea, I realized we had only a little time to enjoy the sandy reef.

We dropped off our bags and headed across the grassy knoll and onto the small shoreline which dipped down to a knee-deep stream of ocean and then up to the large reef. The sky was being painted in orange as the sun began to hide behind wisps of clouds low on the horizon past a little rocky island. It was a beautiful sight, even for a seasoned tropical traveler, but especially for Gib who was bouncing around in joy as per her usual manner.

There were only a few other couples out that evening walking the sandbar and I began to snap pictures of Gib who seemed to magnify the last rays of sunshine to brighten up the entire beach while posing for the pictures like a model against the evening magic hour. That was the high point of my trip, a steep climax and it was all downhill from there, though I had no idea at the time. When the sun finally set and we retired to the hotel embracing like a couple in love, I felt truly comfortable with Gib as if I wanted to spend the rest of the trip or even the rest of my life with her. The moment was fleeting though, and at heart, I was still a sex tourist, and sex tourists aren't supposed to fall in love.

Mark was a typical unhappy American working in an office environment for the first 30 years of his adult life. Now, he was living the dream, working remotely on a tropical island in southern Thailand with his wife of 25 years. Living the dream with his wife of 25 years? For me, I didn't see how those two could possibly go together, and when I showed up at the Indian restaurant in Sala Dan with my hot 25-year-old Thai girl, I felt as if I was guilty of trying to destroy a marriage.

The Indian Restaurant was in a freestanding wood framed building facing one of the side streets. It had an open-air downstairs dining area with wooden tables and plastic chairs, very typical of most of the restaurants in Sala Dan. Outside, there was a grill and two tables with no cover, which we sat down at. In the restaurant, the many young Western tourists went about their business.

I introduced Gib to Mark and his wife Michelle and explained about her limited English. During the dinner, Gib conversed a little with the young Thai waitress, while we had our English conversation.

"So, how much Thai have you learned?" I asked.

"Zip," answered Mark.

"Sawadee Kop[15]?"

"Ok, I know one Thai word, I think, only because they say it every time I walk into the store."

"When do you ever go to the store?" Michelle mocked.

Michelle was an attractive 45-year-old white woman, very fit, tanned, and with bleached blonde hair with one-inch brown roots. They had been in the popular group in high school, gotten together, went to college together, and "worked on their marriage" for 20 years after that. *Gawd... vomit!*

"He doesn't like it much here," she continued. "He just sits in the house and works."

"Well, you're never home, you're always working yourself," he snapped back.

"Always working?" I interjected.

---

[15] Sawadee Kop – Hello for man. Sawadee Ka for woman.

"Yes, that's how it is in Thailand. I work twice as much for about a quarter of the money," Michelle laughed. "I love it though. It's so beautiful here, and the diving is so amazing. There is nothing like this in America, not even in the Caribbean."

"How much do you work?" I asked. This was interesting to me. I could understand moving to Thailand to work remotely with a Western salary, but to go to Thailand to work like a Thai?

"Six days a week, as much as 14 hours per day."

Astonished look.

"It's not as if I'm in the water the whole time!" she laughed. "Lots of the time, I'm sitting at the shop or teaching a dive class."

As dinner went on, and we discussed the finer points of scuba diving, I thought that Mark must get some local pussy on the side while his wife is away for 14 hours. When she finally left for a bathroom break, I just had to find out.

"So, during these 14 hours, have you found yourself a little Thai girl?"

Mark laughed.

"I knew you would say something like that, you and your fuck trips. But no. I'm happily married. I don't really think I could stand one of these Thai girls anyway with their high-pitched voices and tiny frames. And none of them know shit about anything. What kind of conversation could you ever have with one?"

"Oh, I don't know... why bother talking when she could be smoking?" I asked sarcastically.

"Smoking what? Hookah?"

Gib turned away from her conversation toward us.

"You smoke?" Mark asked her.

Gib scowled at him and me and turned back.

I laughed on the inside.

As we were finishing dinner, I realized Mark was the same person that I knew from work many years ago, the same person everyone deals with in American office jobs - overpaid, entitled, and arrogant. In Thailand, he kept himself closed off from the culture that he didn't understand, even though it was his idea to make the move, just to satisfy a desire to get away from a job and city he hated. It wasn't the job, or the city, the problem was him. He blamed all his problems on the people around him and changing his location didn't change that, it only changed the color of the people. Now, he's living in a beautiful place, with a culture that would adore him if he would only smile, but he can't.

Michelle, on the other hand, was the one truly living the dream. She was only a hobby scuba diver prior to the move but had found a true passion in it, living in a beautiful place and showing visitors around its beauty. Her wage of roughly $800/month for working insane hours was like a bonus to her.

"You guys should come diving with me tomorrow!" she exclaimed in a way that Gib understood she was addressing the two of us. "It's a long class in the morning, but I can get you in the water in the afternoon."

Michelle then looked at Gib and said, "Dom Nom?" *or something like that.*

An excited expression came over Gib's face as she glanced at me and then looked back at Michelle and nodded her head excitedly.

Well shit.

So, I really didn't want to go scuba diving. Not only did I not care one bit about looking at fish in the ocean, but I was already tired of the company of boring Westerners, preferring the company of a Thai girl who didn't speak English but would fuck me all day and night. For a moment, the thought hit me that I could fuck her in the ocean while scuba diving, but then I doubted Michelle would leave us alone during our first day of diving. *Cock tease*.

But Gib already had me by the balls apparently and I couldn't say no, so we scheduled a dive at the butt ass crack of dawn, which meant our fuck session that night was tame and we were asleep early.

Boredom. Drunkenness. That was my day lounging around in the Thai dive shop watching my newly crowned flavor of the week learning how to breathe underwater. Thank God, that like any respectable Thai establishment, they had a refrigerator stocked with beer. I entertained the idea of engaging in my first Scuba Dive but when I found out it meant sitting around sober for five hours learning the art of breathing in and breathing out underwater – as if it could be that hard, I chose to be drunk instead. Had I known we would be the only diving customers that day which meant Gib would be getting one-on-one instruction from a Thai, and I'd be forced to sit and converse with my friend's wife, I may have opted to be sober and see some fish.

"She sure is a cutie, are you thinking about marrying her?" Michelle asked.

Oh great, this again.

"Actually, I'm probably going to break up with her as soon as we get back to Pattaya."

Michelle gave me a perplexed and horrified look.

"What's wrong? You two seem to get along so well!" she exclaimed.

"We do, she is a real sweetheart, I could never meet anyone like her back home," I answered.

This is a conversation I've had so many times in my life, I sometimes experiment with different answers knowing the American woman will never understand my point of view regardless.

"Then why would you break up with her?!" she asked.

"So I don't hurt her feelings."

"Breaking up with her won't hurt her feelings?"

"Yes, but not as bad as when I go home."

"Can't you have a long distance relationship?"

"Yes, but why bother if I'm not going to marry her."

"Maybe you will want to marry her later?"

"I can't marry her if she doesn't speak English."

A total lie, I'd rather marry a woman who doesn't speak English. A more truthful statement may have been 'because she might learn English one day.'

"She could learn fast in America!"

"Or, she could get to America and simply find a young Thai man to marry."

"Nathan, don't you want to find true love someday? You'll never find it if you don't give it a chance."

Gee whiz, I've never heard THAT one before. But at least she wasn't giving me the 'you should find someone your own age.'

This conversation went on for hours sitting in that shack of a dive shop until we were ready to get on a boat –

and I was fully inebriated. It was now noon and the tropical sun was beating us all into cinders, even the Thai instructor was complaining about the heat. We boarded a large boat made for bigger groups with long benches running the sides, a bench in the middle and a canopy with the dive tanks and other equipment in the back. I plopped into the middle bench with Gib who was wearing a white tee shirt over her two-piece bathing suit. I took the opportunity to run my hand under it and feel that bubble butt as the boat slipped out of the Sala Dan docks.

Michelle joined us while the Thai instructor steered the boat. Michelle was wearing a one-piece-hide-everything bathing suit that was even further covered by a shoulder to ankle white netted cover-up. My ego couldn't help but compare my success with women to Mark's success. Could I have ever been happy with a woman like Michelle in the states? Honestly, I never had a chance with one, perhaps it was my own fault but I just couldn't see that life as being better than mine, even if my relationships rarely lasted more than a week.

"Excited?" asked Michelle to Gib.

"Ugh!" screamed Gib.

She was as happy as a little girl at Disneyland. It would be her first Scuba dive, but also her first ride in a speedboat, and her first time to hang out with a Western woman. Michelle was being idolized to the point that I felt neglected.

When the time came to get in the water, I was impressed at Gib's relaxed state of excitement. A smile never left her face as Michelle and the instructor got her set up with her mask and tank. I'd imagine too that the attention being placed on her entertainment was a rare treat. Then Michelle equipped herself in a diving mask and tank and sat on the side of the boat with Gib. It was only when the regulator was placed in Gib's mouth that the smile disappeared. Michelle fell off the boat backward and then the instructor helped Gib to do the same and they floated in the water for a moment until some thumbs-up were given and down they went.

I exchanged some pleasantries with the Thai instructor, mostly having to do with the attractiveness of Gib, but I spent most of the hour being apart from her for the first time in over a week debating whether I should break up with her after returning to Pattaya. My stomach grew knots as I examined the various outcomes. Breaking up would be harsh. Here I was showing her the life that well-off Westerners live, of nice hotels, jet-setting across the country, and pure joyful unproductive activities like diving. For the last week, she was living her life in adventure, with anticipation of what each new day would bring.

I could simply take the easy way out and say goodbye to her on my last day, promising to come back as soon as I could and then let us drift apart as I was "too busy" with work. To put another way, *take the chicken-shit way out.*

Or maybe I was just an emotional drunk...

By the time they popped up again, I had worked myself up without any answers and was happy to see her again. After they climbed into the boat and rid themselves of the equipment, Gib turned to me with another expression of pure joy and cuddled herself under my arm for the ride home. For the first time she was lacking energy, the dive took it out of her, but in her limited English explained to me how beautiful it was. *Vewy bootiful.*

The sun was setting as we docked back at Sala Dan and Mark joined us for dinner at a floating restaurant. Koh Lanta had some charm, especially if you like the company of vacationing Westerners. It was a long wooden dock with polished floors and wooden tables, with a selection of fresh seafood about half the cost of similar venues in Pattaya.

The dinner was excruciating for me. The boisterous young kids all around annoyed me. Mark and Michelle with their hypocritical American principals annoyed me. Even Gib annoyed me by giving me no real reason to want to be rid of her. In fact, she was growing more loveable by the day. Michelle had taken a liking to her and the two spent much of the dinner trading words in their respective languages. I mostly drank.

I hid my turmoil behind the image of a drunk ready to pass out and was thrilled when we walked out of the restaurant to say goodbye to my American friends. I hoped to never see them again. Finally, alone with Gib heading to the hotel for some much-needed sex, I calmed down. There is something about going to a hotel to fuck that makes the world a better place.

Gib was a sexy woman in the bed. She was more into it than I was, perhaps a clue as to why she'd had so many kids. It's just something about the way she carried herself. After sex in bed, she'd move her bare ass into my crotch wiggling it slightly while pulling my arm around her in such a way that I'd be horny again. Then the moment she felt any kind of hardening in my dick, she'd turn over and launch into foreplay. Was it all an act? *Who cares.*

I emptied myself into her twice before becoming too exhausted from the long day and slept soundly until the sun woke me in the morning. Then we threw on some clothes and flip-flops and headed downstairs for some breakfast. We were the only guests to arrive so late for breakfast, and we settled into a set of plastic chairs at a plastic table overlooking the little grassy knoll. It was another pleasant day with streams of sun shining through a sparsely clouded sky. Some massages were already being undertaken at the massage hut and Gib sat across the way smiling at me as if I was Brad Pitt.

I really didn't want to do a thing that day, besides get a massage and have a lot of sex. I'd seen enough of the island from the van and the boat to know that it was a typical tropical island, and I wasn't going to find as nice of a place as I was in, at least not with only a day to search. So, when the young Thai in charge of the affairs at the hotel began to put ideas in Gib's head, I wasn't pleased, though I'm sure he meant well.

"What are you guys going to do today?" he asked.

"No plans, just relax," I said.

"Ok. There is a lot to do on the island if you change your mind."

That should have been the end of it, but as is typical being out with a local lady who doesn't speak much English, she wanted to know what was just said and therefore launched into a Thai conversation with him, one that seemed to go on for a while, one that seemed to be destroying my idea of a relaxed day with every word I couldn't understand.

"She wants to go see the cave. It wouldn't take long, it's a nice little trip."

I looked at Gib who was just smiling. Not begging, no puppy dog look, just a smile of knowing that I was going to be taking her to a cave. In her defense, she didn't know I had planned a relaxing day, due to the lack of communication that I was losing patience with.

So, after a really long breakfast – I had to get my relaxing in – we set off on the scooter to find this cave, with Gib driving and myself sitting on back. I normally would never let such an atrocity happen on my vacation but I simply didn't want to do anything that day. Gib was a good driver anyway, probably better than me when it came to dealing with the traffic despite her driving around a man twice her weight. Though really, I'm sure she's driven around two siblings, their kids, and some groceries on a scooter at some point. I've seen scooters with five people on them. After the first couple double-takes, I began to have fun with it, smiling and waving at the young white kids who would snicker.

We eventually got off the busy street and followed some dirt roads into the heart of the island until we came to a small hut that advertised the cave adventure and nature walk. We paid one price of 220 baht for the admission… that's of course 200 baht for me and 20 baht for her. I wonder how this kind of charging would go over back home. "Oh, you are Thai, to go inside, that's $150 for you and $25 for your American friend."

Then we started walking through a jungle. It was a nice walk that followed a stream. I'm not a big nature guy, but Gib's energy transferred to me and I was able to lose my grumpy mood for a while. Until we got to the "cave" that is. It wasn't really a cave, it was more of a hole in the side of a small cliff. I should have known. It's not as if they offered us any flashlights. Even Gib was a little disappointed as we headed away from the "cave" on the trail. But, the little trip would not be totally uneventful.

We passed by a small pool on the stream. It was only 20 feet long and maybe 3 feet deep in the middle caused by some rocks that dammed up the stream. Though it was visible from the trail in one direction, from the other it was mostly shrouded by vegetation so we had not seen it on the way in. Gib stopped on the trail and looked at the pool and then turned to me and giggled. Then she skipped toward the pool.

There are certain situations in the world that don't require language. Gib jumped onto one of the big rocks causing the blockage in the stream, turned around to me with a teasing smile on her face, twerked her hips to one side, and then grabbed the button on her jean shorts. Laughing, she slowly slid down her shorts and panties, removed her shirt and bra, and then backed into the pool with a face inviting seduction.

We seemed to be alone in the jungle, so I happily lost my clothes and joined her. The water was cool and clear, and we had the whole world to ourselves under that canopy of green.

True to Gib's playful character, she slipped my arms the first few times I tried to grab her. She darted around the pool giggling like a kid until I gave up and knelt in the middle waiting for her to come to me. Before that though, she sat on one of the rocks and splashed her feet playfully in the water while leaning her head back enjoying the world. I was envious. Gib seemed to be at the high point of her life when every minute was a thrill.

After she was all kicked out, she laid back on the rock with one leg pointing down in the water toward me and the other splayed out to her side. The result of which was a clear view to her natural pussy, which I couldn't help but make for. I quietly moved through the water until I was close enough to grab her thigh, which startled her. She had become lost in the moment, and probably not horny, I surmised. That should be easily fixable though.

I reached a hand to her pussy and pulled up the hair from her bush until I had a clear view of her clit. She continued to lay sprawled out on the rock when I lowered my mouth to surround her clit for the first time. After massaging her clit a moment, she responded by lifting up on her hands to watch me and slowly grinding her hips.

When I caught some hair in my teeth and stopped to remove it, she smiled and used both her hands to pull apart her pussy lips to give me better access. Her face showed thrill as I plowed my tongue back in. It was the first time I'd gone down on Gib, the first time in years I'd gone down on an unshaved pussy, and I'm pretty sure the first time eating a girl out in the middle of the jungle as well.

It was easily one of the most fun times I've had going down on a girl. Gib was loving it. She stared into my eyes the whole time with a smile on her face, sometimes giggling, and other times moaning and licking her lips, but never closing her eyes. She kept her balance by bracing one leg against a side rock while the other leg continued laying straight into the water. If someone happened down the trail, they'd see a tiny Thai girl sitting on a rock holding her pussy open while the balding head of a farang went to town.

After I'd had enough, Gib slipped down into the water.

"You happy me," she said.

She caught my hard dick with both hands and giggled as she slid herself across my hips. The pool wasn't deep enough for me to stand, if I did I'd have to hold most of her weight, but it was too deep to sit on my ass without drowning, so we ended up fucking in an awkward half knee bend position with me supporting us with one leg and keeping my knee from banging on the rocks with the other. Until we thought better of it and finished off on the throne that was the rock where I went down on her. It was not the most comfortable lay, but fuck it, I just banged an energetic girl half my age in the middle of the jungle in Thailand! Ok, so seeing the cave wasn't so bad as it turned out.

Don't play games with sex workers, end it and move on.

As the sun dawned and the time of absolution grew nearer, my nerves calmed and the answer became clear. As she slept peacefully beside me and the morning sun beamed through the curtains and glistened off her hair, I concluded that it was indeed the softer easier way. I would break up with her upon returning to Pattaya, severing our relationship suddenly. I felt sorry for Gib, but in my own mind, I knew I was doing her a favor. She would learn that farangs come to Pattaya for one thing, her pussy. I would relieve her of the burden of hope when a man goes home promising to see her again and then never fulfilling it. Instead, she could get on with her new career extracting money from pleasure seeking lonely men. Don't play games with sex workers, end it and move on.

For the first time during our transfers back to Pattaya, I was thankful for our language barrier. For the van, plane, bus, and taxi back to the condo, I could only sit alone with my thoughts. Most of them revolved around where I would go the next day that I was free again. The glorious strange pussy!

Though as the taxi made the tedious journey from the bus station to the condo, knots built in my stomach, and my cowardice pleaded with me not to do it, put it off. It's that weak-willed tug at men that leaves them married to the same woman they despise for years, all because they are too scared to put an end to it. I didn't despise Gib though, was it a crazy decision? There was no reason to think I could find a better girl in Pattaya. *Oh dear God, stop being a pussy.*

The taxi stopped and my body lurched in apprehension. My limbs seemed numb as I exited the cab with Gib and the driver and pulled the bags out of the trunk. I handled the payment to the driver and as the taxi pulled away, I looked at Gib standing over our bags with a smile on her face as if to say "Home honey!" *It's now or never.*

I had 15,000 baht prepared in my pocket. I was buying my guilt back from her. I could have left her stranded outside the condo with nothing, but I didn't believe I could have enjoyed the rest of the trip. Besides, that was still far less than I would have paid to daily bargirls over the time I spent with her.

I approached her and pulled the money out so it was clearly visible and produced my best look of disappointment. A look of confusion combined with her never-ending smile. There were few words I could use that she would understand. I grabbed one of her hands and held it with mine while slipping the wad of bills into her palm.

"I'm sorry," I said.

The first look of grief that I'd ever seen on Gib's face appeared as her stubborn smile began to lose its grip. Gazing at the transformation coming over her face, my own heart began to waver.

Go! You idiot!

Gib stood devastated unable to move as I pulled away from her and walked briskly toward the condo with a quick glance over my shoulder to make sure she wasn't chasing, only to see her squatted down on her knees, face in hands, and the money laying on the driveway. I could feel the anguish build in me and knew there was limited time before I would cave and rush back to her.

I entered an open door and sprinted through the eerily empty lobby and into the elevator foyer. Being finally out of sight of Gib and the world, I collapsed on my knees and erupted into tears. I berated myself for my actions. How could I do that? She was a beautiful girl! Perhaps her only flaw was her attraction to me. If Gib had walked into the lobby at that point, I would have thrown my arms around her and professed my undying love. Perhaps we would have stayed together forever having eradicated any courage I had left. Life has plenty of moments such as those, an important life decision made in the heat of emotion. Deep down beneath the agony, my rational self was assured in the outcome of the night.

Gib didn't appear in the lobby that night, yet another clue as to the extent of her character. I imagined her crying for a moment in the driveway before wiping away her tears, grabbing the money and getting on with her life, remembering her silly first farang only as a good time and introduction to the life of Pattaya.

I'm not sure how long I cowered in the foyer bent over fighting tears, but I remember when it ended. A tall overweight American man appeared with a Thai girl in a red one-piece dress half his size and pushed the button.

"She was that good, huh?" he said to me.

"Yes, she was."

I joined them in the elevator and briefly told the story of the breakup.

"I didn't see her out there... she must be over you already," he said.

10

The Seduction of Porn

Squirrel-caging. For the following 24-hours after dumping Gib on the driveway of my condo, the squirrels in my head chased their tails madly in their restrictive little cages. I laid in bed and rehashed every moment of my relationship with Gib, from what I could have done differently when I met her at the massage parlor to all the times I could have broken it off sooner. Why did I spend so much time with her? Why did I get so close? I resented her for becoming attached to me despite her being a pseudo-sex worker. I resented myself for getting close to her, and even more, I resented myself for not being the type of man to love a single woman and settle down. I would be a lucky man to spend even a couple of years with her.

As I moped around my condo for the entire day, I looked for excuses to get out, to find a streetwalker somewhere and manhandle her, to hate-fuck all my self-pity away in one glorious assault. In my mind, it wasn't myself that was the problem, it was Pattaya. I was resentful and angry.

Never put a bargirl ahead of a friend.

Eventually, my thoughts turned to Porn, my first real interest of the trip and remembering the moment with her when she discovered my plans to lavish Gib in travel, I knew I could take her if I put in the effort. I began to rehearse what I would say at the bar until I remembered that Ben was always there, and besides, of all the friends I made while on sex vacations, he seemed to be one that I certainly didn't want to break my rule about messing with his girls. He could crush me with a single swipe of one of those massive limbs.

My brain unconsciously began searching for excuses to ignore the rule until remembering the encounter in the hallway when I brought Gib home for the first time, already considering her a girlfriend of sorts. Ben had grabbed her ass as if she was an object. He'd already broken the unspoken rule between sex tourists, he'd already moved in on one of my girls. Not only had he trespassed on my turf, but he'd also done it to one of the few unblemished souls in the city. He didn't deserve any loyalty from me. If anything, he needed to be taken down a few pegs.

By that evening, I had become a predator, a self-absorbed pig prepared to destroy others to release the confusion that I had bottled up. I texted Ben to find out what he was up to and to discover his whereabouts.

"Single again mate? Damn! Come over, I'm at the condo with a skank!"

There could not have been a better answer. I texted back that I'd sit this one out but meet him for lunch the next day. Then, I put on my best clothes and quietly opened the door and tiptoed down the hall.

There was not an ounce of apprehension in my body as I moved through the crowded night streets of the sex capital of the world. My mission was simple, to despoil Porn of her high horse that she strode around on in that bar pretending to be too good for sex tourists. I'd do the exact thing I loathed of other men, I'd tell her exactly what she wanted to hear and then treat her like the whore that she was.

As I approached the British Bar, I noticed the usual suspects including Farang Bob, the other miserable British drunks, and the unmistakable short black ponytail sitting atop the sexy black and white striped dress hunched over to caress the pocketbook away from an oblivious random sex tourist. This was no time to be coy, I strode straight to the empty seat next to her and ordered a beer in a loud enough voice to turn her attention.

"Nathan! What are you doing here? Where is Gib?" she asked.

There was some excitement in her face. For the first time, we could engage each other without the overbearing presence of Ben.

"I broke up with her, I just couldn't handle the lack of communication. I want a girl I can talk to," I answered.

I had prepared the response. I knew I had to convince her the breakup was something other than typical farang bullshit.

"Oh no! She's such a nice girl!"

"And I'm crazy about you! Just like every man here."

Porn put her hand over her mouth and looked away for a moment. My response seemed to shock her, despite obviously hearing the same nonsense all day. Was I too direct?

"Wait, honey! I have drink."

The chubby European sitting on the other side of her was growing annoyed with every word between us, which was my intention. His only choice at that point would be to give up or offer to barfine her, the latter of which would be denied, and I'd have Porn to myself.

I ordered my own beer and waited for her to finish her drink with a man who was now rightfully feeling threatened. I sneered at the conversation they were having and the glances in my direction. Though he may never know it, I was doing him a favor anyway as Porn would have unloaded drinks all night on him and then declined to seal the deal, sending him packing with a woody poking through his shorts and no choice but to spend even more on another girl not even half as charming.

With her drink dry, it seemed he intended to keep buying anyway, possibly a bit of ego to keep what he thought was his, but it was Porn who declined. She put her hand on his shoulder and said in a very professional manner, "I'm sorry honey." She turned away and I shrugged my shoulders at the pathetic loser who was just rejected by a girl he thought would go with any man who had money.

The instant Porn turned to face me, I knew she would be leaving the bar with me that night. It was a look I'd never seen from her towards any of the other men in the bar. It was a look of genuine interest. Her eyes were wide and her smile beamed like a high school girl with a crush. It seemed as if she'd sat in that bar for all those days just to arrive at that moment, with a man she considered worthy of her time and capable of treating her like a real farang's girlfriend.

I smiled back, and she blushed for a second and lunged forward clinching her arms around my neck. As my face smothered in her hair, I wrapped my own arms around her in a way to get a sense of the form of her body. I got aroused at the firmness of her body wrapped up in that tight dress.

"I can't believe it! I think Gib so good for you and you are so nice!" she said.

"I know, I feel bad," not really a lie.

"How was Koh Lanta? I really want to go there someday!"

"Maybe I will take you," I answered. Total lie.

"Yea sure!"

"Well, I don't want to go to Koh Lanta again, but I've never been to Phuket and I might go there before I go home," I said. Total lie.

"Oh! Phuket very beautiful! I want to go there too but no one ever take me!"

"Have you ever had sex on the beach?" I asked.

"NO! Oh, scary."

"Why scary?"

"Because someone will see!"

"What if I will take you to Phuket if you have sex on the beach with me?" charming in my own mind.

"Nathan! So bad!"

"I know," not a lie.

I hesitated for as long as I could in buying her a drink, mainly because I didn't think it would be necessary, but eventually the pestering from the old Thai bartender was too distracting. It did provide a segue into something I'd been wanting to ask her though.

"So, all these drinks you sell and no one has ever seen you leave with a man. Do you ever barfine?" I asked.

"I don't like, but I have before. Only very nice guys!"

"Bob isn't nice?" I asked motioning in his direction. He'd been trying not to show his interest in us since I arrived at the bar.

"Oh! MY GOD! I think I die!"

"What about Ben?" I continued.

"Ben is nice, but he's so big! I think he hurt."

"He won't hurt you, you're right, he's very nice once you are alone with him."

"But I'm very small, small pussy! You know!"

I laughed.

"He's not that big."

"How you know!?"

"I was only joking, maybe you are right." Lie... *Because we picked up a bargirl and double penetrated her one night.*

We conversed over drinks for about an hour as we became closer, with me playing the nice guy who had lost his heart to a girl in a bar until her body was leaned into me with her arms draped around my neck as if we were a couple. I moved my hand down to her ass to feel her solid definition. She wasn't quite as round as Gib but firmer and lacking the baby fat. I was ready to throw her down on the floor of the bar and really give Farang Bob something to be jealous about.

"So, would you like to get out of here and grab a real dinner?" I asked.

"Yes!" answered Porn.

"How much is the barfine?"

"Oh Nathan, it's ok, I'm off work already. I don't want you barfine me," she said. *Music to my ears.*

Maybe she thought I'd give her extra money, or maybe she truly thought she was going to be my girlfriend. That is something I'll never know. What I do know is that for Porn not to be required a barfine meant she was truly special in that bar, regardless of the hours of her shift. If she met a farang at the bar, there would be a barfine, simple as that. The alternative is she was willing to pay it to go out with me so it wouldn't feel like a barfine, or she intended to never go back to work.

Unlike go-go bars, there was no locker room for her to change into, she simply grabbed her purse from behind the bar and journeyed down the road with me, much to Farang Bob's displeasure. I tried not to make eye contact. 'What does he have that I don't have?' I could feel him muttering to himself. The answer to that would be a touch of class, not a ton, but exponentially more than you.

"I'm so happy you take me!" she said.

"I'm so happy you came with me," I answered. Sort of a lie. I was happy that I'd be getting a feel of that pussy in a short time whereas so many other men did not, but I really couldn't care about anything more.

"How about the food court?" I asked, we were walking that direction anyway.

"I don't like." *Ugh.*

"Ok ok, I was only joking! How about Leng Kee on Central?" Lie. I wouldn't have been joking if she said ok.

"Oh yes! You make me so happy, Nathan!" she exclaimed.

And she did seem happy. I was getting a sense of guilt for the night she was about to enjoy. There would be no relationship, no trips to Phuket, she was going to be tossed out of the condo right after I had my way with her. I couldn't help but wonder why I was finding it so easy to get a girlfriend in Pattaya though. Weren't we all there for sex? I decided it would be her own fault to get her hopes up so easily for a man she knew so little of... if fact, one of the few pieces of information she had about me was a propensity for dumping girls.

We made the short walk down the alley to Soi Buakhao and over to Central where the restaurant was. The streets were hopping that night and we blended in with the multitudes of other 50-year-old Westerners with their young bargirl toys. Nothing to see here.

The waitress at Leng Kee seemed to recognize me, as if to say, I hope this one can help you order off the menu a little easier. She could. The experience dining with Porn was a stark contrast to dining with Gib. With Gib, I had to handle everything the way a Westerner would if he were by himself, but Porn was amazing. She was smart and could translate well and even helped make recommendations. It begged the question.

"Did you go to college?"

"I'm going to college now, I want to be nurse." *Just wow.*

"You're amazing," I said. Not really a lie.

"Thank you!" she laughed. "I want to meet a nice man and travel. I don't want to stay here."

"So, you are working in the bar to pay for school?"

"Yes, my family very poor. I want to help them, too."

You must be a sex tourist to know just how rare this sort of interaction is. You'd think it would be commonplace. You'd think that poor girls with no options to pay for school would resort to selling themselves as a temporary solution, but the reality is that the mindset you need for selling your body is exactly opposite the one that would desire to go to school. Porn had found an elegant solution, she sold drinks and took money from sex tourists without selling herself too often, or at least being very picky about it.

It also better explained her attraction to me. She was after bigger and better things, she needed a husband to marry to ferry her away to countries where being a nurse meant good money. She may have felt more comfortable with me than the other drunks at the bar, but she also considered her opportunities were far more lucrative and therefore worth opening her legs for.

"And I want to help you!" I said. Miserable lie.

"Really?" she asked looking at me with starry eyes. "It's ok though, I like you."

Dining with Porn was a real pleasure. If I had been in the same state of mind as when I met Gib, that night, and the rest of the trip, and possibly the next few years of my life would have turned out much differently. As it was though, I was only getting more excited about the hideous number I was about to do on her. Now, I wasn't just

199

seducing a struck-up bargirl, but a stuck-up college girl. That's something I didn't have much success at in my own college days.

By the time we arrived back at the condo building, we were all over each other. It never ceases to amaze me the passion a 20-year-old Thai girl can lay upon a farang over twice her age. Just to get her inside faster, I picked her up to carry her into the elevator as she screamed. For the ride up, I let her down and held her small waist close for a long smooch. She had thin lips, but she knew how to use them in long caresses guided by a wet tongue.

Arriving at my floor, I calmed things down a bit.

"Shhh, my neighbors get really mad about noise." The last thing I wanted was Ben poking his head out.

Halfway down the hall, mere feet from Ben's door…

"Honey, I think you got me drunk!"

I closed my eyes expecting the hairless yeti to appear, as her voice was unmistakable and even through the closed door, Ben would have identified his Pattaya love. I concluded he was likely picking up another skank while I was about to enjoy the only forbidden fruit east of Second Road. For good measure, though, I shuffled the laughing Porn down the hall and into my condo.

"Oh, very nice! I never been here, honey!"

Inside, the slender body meandered toward the glass door to the balcony with me following and my eyes trained on the bulge in the back of her dress. She opened the door and leaned against the railing, with her breasts resting on the top, and her head draped forward peering joyfully over the city that was her home, the city she had tamed where so many girls were enslaved.

I approached her and connected my body to hers, wrapping an arm around her shoulders and resting the other hand on her hip, and leaning in where our cheeks met, I felt her energy flow into me. That sudden urge of love, of a connection with a female, that drives men crazy in all parts of the world, was an obstacle to my mission. In that moment, I looked into her eyes and didn't see an object, I saw a person. I saw a beautiful girl who was discovering the world and still believed in all the dreams we tell children, of a world that will give her everything she wants. In that moment, I wanted to help her find her dreams.

I wrenched my gut back under my control, dropped my gaze from her loveable smile to the mounds on her chest, and refocused myself. I pushed my crotch into her butt and slowly ground to bring an erection.

Porn laughed. "I need to shower. I smell!"

I pushed in for another smooch, this time holding her cheek to force her mouth into mine, so I could stick my tongue deep in her mouth. It was a raunchy kiss, not a kiss of love, though I'm not sure she noticed.

"Hurry up!" I said, running my hand down to her breasts and dragging her away from the balcony.

We retreated to the bathroom where I couldn't wait to see the dress come off for the first time.

"No Nathan! I'm shy!" *yea, saw that coming.*

I had to figure out a way around the shy girl and no shower together routine. Pulling her clothes off and simply refusing to leave was the best strategy I had.

"Ahh, stop it!" she yelled.

She was a little shell-shocked when I whipped her dress over her head in one smooth motion, but she was still in loving-life mode. A slap was forthcoming, but then she laughed and kissed me more. We were a couple, after all, it was ok to be seen naked.

Now with only her panties left, I finally laid eyes on the sight that she protected more than any other girl in Pattaya. There are Thai bodies and then there was Porn's. She was right to hold it in reserve, a weapon to use only on men where its full effect could be realized. Her breasts were perfect in proportion to her body, her hips slim but with a layer of skin that made her appear sensual, and her waist was a perfect 7/10 the size of her hips giving her the most desirable of hourglass shapes. Her skin, normally hidden from the sun under her dress, was free of tattoos, scars, or other blemishes and carried a fair Asian complexion the color of the inside shell of a coconut. Her only defects, if you were being picky, was the heavily defined tan lines just above her knees and below her shoulders and neck separating the brown portion of her body exposed to the sun every day from working in an outside bar.

"It's ok, let me see you," I said.

I slowly grabbed her panties and pulled them down to reveal a shaved pussy below a ridge of defined muscle at the base of her caved-in belly.

When my trance wore off, I looked up to see a somewhat confused look on her face. She wasn't fighting to push me from the bathroom, but I believe she may have begun to get a clue that I was only after one thing. I figured it was too late at that point for her to do anything about it, but I didn't have a ton of experience in those spots, and instead decided to camouflage my intentions a little while longer.

"You are the most beautiful girl I've ever seen," I said. *Not a lie.*

The side of her mouth curled up to replace her puzzled look, and I stood up to kiss her and remove my clothes. I started the shower and we continued our foreplay under the hot water in the cramped space. Her resistance to showering together was gone and she was even enjoying it, though I had to maneuver her hands to the parts of my body I wanted her to wash. As she got the message and lathered up her hands and stroked my crotch, I instantly grew rock hard, and I began to lose myself in the moment.

I guided her down, practically pushing her shoulders like a street whore who wasn't cooperating. No recoil.

When that gorgeous face was at the level of my dick, I saw a receptive look, and with her eyes staring into mine, her mouth opened, and I slid myself into her mouth. She massaged me with her lips creating a sort of ring slipping up and down my shaft, like a girl who rarely gives blowjobs.

I could feel my face droop as I fought the urge to grab the back of her head and jam my dick down her throat. It might have been worth it, but I couldn't expect her to continue into the bedroom if I did, so instead of receiving a terrible blowjob in the shower which may be souring her desire, I motioned to her to stand back up after less than a minute. She seemed relieved.

"I never do before," she said. *Now, who's lying?*

"Never?"

"No, never."

"What about boom-boom? You've done that before right?"

"Of course, Nathan. I'm not virgin!"

"Well then, let's go boom-boom!"

I stopped the shower, and we began drying off, though I grabbed her while we were both still dripping and carried her into the bedroom, again bringing her to giggles.

I tossed her on the bed like a toy and she scooched to the pillow with her knees in the air and slightly spread with her arms outstretched begging for me to come to her. In the light from the city, I could make out the definition of her closed-lip pussy and budding clit. I wondered if she was wet enough to just plow in.

She wasn't.

"Ow! Slow down!"

Without any self-control, I found myself smashing the head of my dick into her pussy like a rapist. Her tight dry pussy walls were putting up enough friction to keep me from sliding in and I began working my dick in and out with one hand while holding myself up with the other, all the while ignoring her pleas to take it easy.

"Nathan! Wait! Slowly!"

Finally, my dick had plunged in far enough to release some of her internal juices and the movement became less labored.

"What tha fuck?!"

I knew at the very least the scowl on her face meant her opinion of me was altered. I was not the caring man she thought I was, but fortunately, there was no more pain for her and I began sliding my body back and forth over hers, enjoying every contact my body made from my knees to my dick coursing in and out to my nipples running over hers. I sloppily shoved my tongue in her mouth to which she was not completely unreceptive since she was likely fighting a bit of confusion.

When that became boring, I lifted up on my arms and gave her a mean pound, and when her legs squeezed a bit to stop me from pounding her again, I thrust with all my energy as fast as I could.

"Slowly, please! I don't have sex a lot," she moaned.

Her legs managed to keep me from the full-on pounding I was attempting, and when she reached up to pull me close to her, shades of my first awful encounter in Pattaya popped into my head. No more being controlled by Pattaya bargirls, I thought as I grabbed her biceps and pushed her arms down beside her.

Then I moved my right leg over her left so she could no longer get leverage on my hips, and proceeded to thrust inside her as deep as I could using her arms to hold her body in place.

"Nathan! Slow down," she moaned.

She turned her head to the side and moaned in muted displeasure, sometimes squenching her face.

I took a good look at her body as my orgasm began to build.

"Not inside please," she whispered still with her head turned.

"Ok."

I didn't want to cum inside her anyway, though I almost changed my mind when she said that. However, I may have been a heartless bastard at the time, I still had enough decency not to completely derail the poor girl from her goals by giving her a child.

In not a micro-second to spare, I climbed up to her face and let my cum spurt onto her cheek... because I missed.

"Ah God!" she yelled and craned her neck away as far as she could while fighting my weight.

The rest of my cum found its way on her neck and hair, and I rolled off onto my back and stared at the ceiling, fully satisfied.

"Good God, that's what you like?" she whimpered as she retreated to the bathroom to clean herself.

Wondering what she would do, I didn't feel any pity for her. She did, after all, jump into bed with a man she barely knew. If it was a straight paid-for sexual encounter, she could simply collect her money and go, but it wasn't.

I was a little surprised when she came back to bed, still naked, and laid down next to me, although her smile was nowhere to be found.

"Did you do that with Gib? Fuck her like that?" she asked.

"No."

"Why me?" *ah, what a question.*

I glanced at her, the smell of my cum permeating the room and somehow taking her beauty down several levels.

"Because Gib adored me. You just want a fucking plane ticket."

I believe with that statement, she realized the truth, and quietly went about getting dressed and leaving my condo.

I'm not sure if I was correct in my assessment of her. Dealing with girls in Thailand is confusing to me because of the differences in perception. She was definitely after a plane ticket, a new way of life, but she may not have known herself well enough to understand that was the underlying motive. She may simply have been responding to her emotions that saw me as a provider, a man who could

206

elevate her and love her at the same time. She probably wasn't a cold calculating gold-digger, she was only following what her heart told her it wanted.

I could have slept that night cuddled up with a sensual young girl who treated me like a rock star, but instead, I slept alone, and barely slept at all, knowing there would be a price to pay for the night I had. I hoped the price would be nothing more than an awkward conversation with Ben, but as I sat in my condo the next morning, drinking instant coffee, and watching my phone for Ben's text, I could feel there would be more of a reckoning than a small bro spat over a bargirl.

Might as well get on with it.

I walked with Ben to the food court for the first time since I had met Gib while debating how I should break the news to him. I knew it would be far better to tell him myself, possibly in the form of a brag, but I couldn't bring myself to do it, as Ben made me feel like a sex tourist again, just a guy in Pattaya to have fun with whores.

"Awesome, mate! Single again! We going to find some tramps tonight or what?"

"That does sound awesome." *It truly did.*

"Can't believe you didn't come over last night. I had this girl from beach road in my condo. 1,000 baht. She'd do anything, mate. That's the only reason I picked her up. Get this…

"I was just walking down Beach Road and this girl was trying to sale herself to this big Indian. She was saying, 'anything you want, fuck my ass, no condom.' She was tweaking or something, nervous as fuck. I just stopped to watch the show.

"But when the Indian walked away, well... 'I'll take that, girly!'"

"So, you fucked her in the ass with no condom?" I asked.

"Hell yea, mate, and she road my cock in her ass like a champ. She straight bounced on it like she'd done it a million times. Wouldn't suck it afterward though," he laughed.

"Ben, do you WANT to die of Aids?"

"Ahh, I don't worry about it. I don't fuck ladyboys."

"Maybe not, but do you think the guys out there fucking ladyboys in the ass are only fucking ladyboys? I've even met an old man that would put his dick anywhere."

"Did he have Aids?" Ben asked.

"Maybe. He said 'heart' problems."

"Ah, come on, mate. Don't stress me out!"

I laughed my way through our conversation knowing he'd much rather have had my night.

"So, what did you do last night, just sit in your condo and cry over Gib?" he laughed.

"Not exactly."

"So, what did you do?"

"I'll tell you on the way to the bar."

Why I even intended to go to the bar, I have no idea. It's as if none of the decisions I made since arriving in Pattaya were sound, but as I found myself walking the short distance to the bar, we both seemed to have forgotten that I was supposed to tell a story. My brain was frozen in apprehension.

My legs were numb as I stepped into the space that constituted the British Bar, while Ben strode up to the counter, oblivious that any trouble was brewing and ordered his usual.

I noticed Farang Bob sitting at the opposite corner, and when the ponytail of Porn whipped around from the seat next to him, a very justifiable panic set in as Farang Bob's face turned to a scowl.

"Ben, I changed my mind, I'm not going to stay here," I said to him standing just back from the bar counter.

"Yea, sorry, I'll explain later," and I turned to head out.

"Hey!" Farang Bob yelled at me having closed the distance faster than I could realize.

I hadn't been in a real fight since college, and I thought all of that macho stuff was well behind me, but I was not lacking self-defense skills. In fact, the one maneuver I had executed a few times, was about to get more practice.

I turned to face the oncoming onslaught and felt the fat paw of Farang Bob at my throat. In response, I reached my hand over and grabbed the meaty portion of his palm and twisted his arm with everything I had while grabbing his elbow.

For a second, I had control of the big guy, his body bent at the waist as my leverage on his arm subdued him, but that moment did not last as the momentum of his body, perhaps thirty percent bigger than mine pushed me back into one of the few tables and he was able to sidestep my grip and fall into me. The table fell one way while I went the other, with his disgusting body falling on top. I pulled my arms up to protect myself from the thrashing that was sure to come.

Thank God for me, Ben was not all bluster. Before any blows were landed, he had Bob off me and onto his side.

"Hey, fuck you!" Bob yelled at me. "I'll fucking kill you, you mother fucker!"

"Calm down, what the fuck!" Ben yelled, having Bob completely subdued.

"Alright, alright," Bob said as he quit fighting.

Then I could hear the voice of Porn standing over us. "Yea, fuck you!" she yelled at me.

Ben was letting Bob to his feet as he realized this had something to do with Porn.

"What the fuck, Porn?" he asked.

"He's fucking asshole."

Ben looked at me. I was regaining my composer and I looked back at him and shrugged. "I fucked her, came on her face, and then threw her out. Meant to tell you before we got here."

Bob lunged at me again and Ben instinctively blocked his attack. I was amazed at Ben's physical ability to shut him down as if he was a child. Some Thai men also showed up out of nowhere and began to corral the big Brit. The Thai lady behind the bar began yelling, "get out, all of you."

"Yea, let's go," said Ben menacingly toward me.

I wasn't sure if I was going to get the rest of the beating from Ben going back to the condo, but I nevertheless walked with him. Maybe I deserved it anyway.

"So, how the hell did you fuck Porn?" he asked.

I relayed the whole night to him as well as I could, not leaving out any details. Ben listened and walked coolly beside me.

"Can't believe you got her in bed."

"You're not pissed?"

"Well, definitely a little… But, you know what, fuck her, mate. I've been trying to fuck her for months and she just jumps in bed with you because you offer her a vacation in Phuket? What a cunt."

Getting attacked by a jealous sex tourist over a bargirl… there's always a first for every trip. I wondered if the little show would finally earn him her pussy, but somehow, I doubted it. As for Ben, it seemed his disrespect for all the girls in Pattaya extended even to Porn. We became good friends after the incident and even after my vacation was over. Guess I had my own learning to do… a rule that Ben embodied. Never put a bargirl ahead of a friend.

11

What's Up Blood Sucker

"I'm going to Walking Street tonight," I said to Ben the next afternoon.

I chuckled at the ridicule on Ben's face. He thought of Walking Street as nothing but an overpriced way to get the same experience as elsewhere in the city. I agreed with him to an extent, but I also expected the bargirls there to be more attractive than their Soi 6 or Soi LK Metro counterparts.

In reality, I simply wanted to head the opposite direction from the condo, a fresh start, a place that might give me the bargirl experience I'd so far been lacking.

"Well, I leave you to it, mate," said Ben. "I'm going to go talk to Porn, see what the fuck. Afterward, I may go ass fuck some Soi 6 skank."

Now, it was me with the look of ridicule. Just what was it with that girl?

"You should come with me, if Farang Bob is there, we can take him somewhere and beat the shit out of him."

I had hardly thought of Farang Bob since he attacked me the previous day. He was just a little brain – a man that lets women control all his actions and emotions. Women and alcohol anyway. It was Porn who tried to pummel me that day in the bar, Bob was merely her tool, no different than if she'd been holding a hammer.

I felt Ben was dwelling on it, perhaps feeling inadequate after discovering she wasn't so hard to get into bed after all, though he didn't seem to be placing any blame on me. For all the negative opinions I had of him, the absurdity of putting bargirls ahead of friends was not one of them.

One thing was certain though, I was going nowhere near the British Bar for the rest of my trip. Not because of Farang Bob, but because of Porn. If she could persuade a dumb farang to attack another one over her pussy, just what else was she capable of? Getting drunk all afternoon has never been my thing on sex trips anyway.

So, I bid Ben farewell and relaxed at the rooftop condo pool until the sun began to set, building up in my mind the still unknown stunning bargirl I would pick up that night. I hadn't yet found my one-per-trip supermodel bargirl yet. Porn was almost in that class, but she exuded a bit too much girl-next-door. Now, I wanted to put any money concerns aside and find a trophy, a girl who would be reserved for only the super wealthy or handsome young men if she wasn't a whore.

When men think of Pattaya, they usually think of Walking Street. Many who travel to Pattaya may not even be aware of all the other venues for buying pussy, and because of that, the clubs on Walking Street are nicer and more expensive, catering to tourists without a clue or with too much money.

I passed under the giant marque of Walking Street at 8 pm on the dot, alone amongst the sea of tourists -- men seeking companionship, couples from various countries sightseeing, and Asian tour groups marching behind a leader holding a sign. Door girls from a few of the go-go bars stood outside in partially revealing clothing, posing for the occasional raised smartphone. Street performers from guys on stilts, to break dancers, to artists groveled for the scraps of wealth from the passing mob.

Call down the girl you want, don't wait for the girl that finds you.

I ducked down an alley on the left, with the destination of Sapphire Club in mind. An upscale club as far as I knew based on their social media presence, I figured it a good choice to find my dream girl.

Upon entering the double doors and stepping inside, my dreams came true, at least for a moment. Sapphire is a cozy club with a rectangular stage dominating the center. Typical to Thai go-go bars, a line of young girls stood on the edges displaying themselves for the club's sparse patrons. The girls wore skimpy black shorts with a white top displaying the Sapphire name. Of the twenty or so girls lined up, I counted at least five that I would consider in my dream girl category with over half of the rest being squarely in my range of doable.

I had a seat towards the side when a Thai waiter approached to get my drink order... a dude, really? Sapphire was the opposite of what I was used to in go-go bars, completely laid back and non-pushy. So much so that I wondered if I appeared as a customer not worth the trouble. *Ignore him, maybe he will leave*, they thought? I'm sure I was overreacting.

I sat on the plush bench staring at the girls on stage, practically lost as to how to act, realizing that for the whole trip I'd yet to go to a go-go bar. I felt as if I was right off the plane. It may have even been refreshing to get approached by some hideous girl trying to make her whole night worth it by scoring a drink.

When the group of girls rotated off the stage, passing by me and avoiding eye contact, an even more astonishing group took their positions. One girl I recognized, she had long flowing blonde hair, a tall slender body with large silicone breasts. Lala, I knew her from the Sapphire Facebook page. Surreal, seeing her standing next to all the other dancers, for in my mind she felt as if an untouchable model, a woman that most of the population of men in the world would only see in media.

My body slumped, as a feeling of inadequacy overcame me. *What the fuck? She's just a whore.*

I searched myself as to why I couldn't call her down and have a conversation. It'd be easy, something I'd done dozens of times in my life, a conversation between a bargirl and her prospective customer. Surely, she was waiting on a customer better than me, I thought.

Why those thoughts overcame me at that moment, I couldn't tell you. The reality is I probably would have been her dream customer, a nice 50-year-old man with money to spend. Call down the girl you want, don't wait for the girl that finds you.

I paid my tab for the single drink and left Sapphire.

I stomped across the small alley to the next club, *What's Up*.

Inside those sets of double doors was a strikingly different scene from Sapphire. It was more festive, more in-your-face. Men sat on the white couches with girls draped across them, drinks piled on the tables. The girls ran around flirting and teasing whether it was their customer or not. If I had been in a normal state of mind, or more to the point,

215

not acting like an amateur sex tourist, I would have turned right around and went straight back to Sapphire to call Lala off the stage. As it were though, my choices were to no longer be mine very shortly…

A waitress grabbed my arm and ushered me to one of the empty chairs on a side wall, and as I was making the walk, I caught the stare of a girl standing next to the stage who had been huddled in a group as I entered.

A real beauty. She was 23-years-old, with a petite, mature body wrapped in an elegant white dress. Her natural breast molded the top of her hourglass silhouette while a perfectly proportioned ass rounded out the bottom half. Her straight black hair was pulled back in a ponytail so as not to hide her exquisite facial features, sexy pointed eyes and lush full lips with a smile of straight white teeth.

She might have known me to be a mark from that moment as she pointed a finger and nodded her head as if to say, "I'm going to come there, and you are going to buy me drinks."

She plopped in the booth next to me, put her hand on my chest, tilted her head, and smiled coyly.

"You ready for some fun, handsome?"

I was.

Her English was very good, not quite the vocabulary of Porn, but I knew she'd been conversing in English for years.

She leaned her breast against my arm and rubbed my belly while peering into my eyes seductively. Her movements were elegant, her look confident, she had me broken from the first pearly white smile as if an animal handler… a John-whisperer.

When the waitress appeared, she turned and nodded her head and extended her finger ordering a drink, without my permission. *I guess I was buying her a drink*.

"And what would you like, handsome?"

The handsome's were out in full force in this club, and I was lapping it all up. I was grinning like a stooge, playing the part, the part of a tourist with too much money.

"I'm Nok, what's your name?" she asked, somewhere into the 2nd or 3rd drink.

Unbeknownst to me at the time, Nok was a star of that club, a featured dancer and one of the highest earners. What's Up pays its dancers well, but it requires much in return. For their weekly salary, they had a minimum number of drinks to sell, including bonuses for girls who sell the most, of which Nok would often win. Extracting money from men was her business, and she excelled at it, the exact type of sex worker I make a point to avoid.

To her credit, she was a blast to buy drinks for, though she acted like a socialite at a club rather than a sex worker, she gave me her undivided attention with every drink, acting like she was having as much fun as I. Maybe she was, with her cut of the 200 baht drink, she'd pocketed 500 baht from me by the time I tired of the handouts.

"Can I barfine you?" I asked.

Her expression turned to business, seemed she would have been happy to drink the night away in the club, it's as if I surprised her with the question.

"Short-time or long-time?" she asked.

"Which would you prefer?"

Always find out if the girl wants to stay the night before agreeing to a long-term barfine. More likely than not, a bargirl will accept the extra money for an all-nighter

217

but may intend to leave as soon as possible. If you end up with a girl like this, you can make her your prisoner, but seriously, what's the point? It's easier to determine beforehand how long they wish to stay.

"Short-time is ok," she said.

"3,000," I stated.

I knew the moment I said the price, I had handicapped her in the negotiation, she intended to quote higher but discovered I knew the rate already.

"Ok," she said.

Nok spoke to the waitress and relaxed against the couch with her legs and arms crossed. It wasn't party time anymore, it was work time. The butterflies in my belly, knowing I'd soon have this amazing woman in my bed, conflicted with my apprehension that she'd be no good, as I watched her sitting beside me bored from the routine.

"Where are you staying?" she asked.

"The BASE condo. You know it?" I asked.

"No, I don't know. You have condo here?" she asked, her interest peaked.

"I'm only renting for a month," I replied.

"Oh, very nice!" she said.

A middle-aged Thai lady appeared at our booth and sat down. She could have been Nok's mother, with the similar demeanor and beauty.

"Ok, so you want to barfine her? Short-time?"

"Yes," I said.

The lady glanced at Nok, who jerked her hand up and extended three fingers. I swear I caught a scowl on her face. *That would be the one and only time I got the best of her.*

"Can you pay now?" she asked.

Never pay a barfine up front if you can keep from it. I wasn't sure if I could or not and forked over the cash, at which point Nok left to get dressed while the mama-san sat with me.

"She's nice girl, she not barfine too much, you're lucky," she said. *Yea Sure.*

"Why doesn't she barfine much?" I asked.

"This club expensive. Most customers only drinking."

I settled all the tabs with the mama-san, with a whopping total of 5,000 baht. Astonished at the price tag, I was not accustomed to Walking Street clubs, and I meticulously went over all the bill, sure they had added a few drinks. They hadn't. Nok was a stunning woman, but worth 3x as much as I had paid for Suda? *Maybe she was. Dear lord, please save me.*

When Nok appeared in her street clothes, all I could think was, "God Bless Thailand." She was an angel in her club clothes, but in that state, all the girls are like caricatures. To see her in a tight-fit white tank top and jean shorts so my brain naturally compared her to all the women in the world, I realized her true beauty. She was a 1 in 10,000 girl.

"Ok, are you ready?" she asked.

I followed her out the door and we strode side-by-side to the end of the alley not saying much. I sighed at the impersonal nature of it, though I suppose I didn't expect much at the time. Men drooling over her was her whole world, she didn't need to put in any effort, and I resigned myself to a stuck-up bargirl experience.

"Ok, I follow you," she said, jumping on the back of a motorbike taxi. She wouldn't even share a bike with me.

In my years of buying pussy, I've experienced a range of attitudes on that first encounter, from girls who turned their head avoiding eye contact the whole time to nymphos who craved dick more than I craved pussy. I couldn't categorize that first time with Nok. Stuck-up? For sure, but it felt as though she was playing hard-to-get, rather than too-good-for-me.

She strode confidently into my condo ahead of me, her hips swaying back and forth as if posing for an audience on both sides. Her eyes darted around. The condo lights glistened off her exposed neck inviting me to rush in, to attack her, but I couldn't, only she could initiate.

She continued her round of the condo, inspecting the balcony where Porn had nearly entranced me a day earlier, but showing little interest in the view over Pattaya. She flipped the lights on in the bedroom but never passed the plane of the door. Reaching the bathroom, she poked her head inside while I stood fixated on her ass bunched up in her tight jean shorts, and her smooth fair-skinned legs leaned against the door frame. Finally, she acknowledged my presence.

"Ok, you shower first," she said.

She relaxed on the couch as I washed. While standing in the water, I tried to psyche myself up for the session. My aggressiveness from the night with Porn was gone, perhaps scared out of me by Farang Bob. The only plan I had was to treat her with the utmost respect, which a bargirl in her class demanded.

She was ready to jump in as I toweled off but still waited for me to leave before undressing.

"Wait in bedroom, I'll be quick," she said.

So, I climbed under the covers naked in the bedroom almost dreading the shower to cutoff and her appearance to service me. I believed there was no chance the sex would be good. I expected her to clamber into the bed, situate herself next to me and command me to climb on, while she daydreamed about her young Thai boyfriend, or played with her phone. *I'd be so wrong...*

With the bedroom lights still on, she appeared with a towel wrapped around her breast and a smile, a big smile even, as if she enjoyed herself. She stepped onto the bed and stood over my ankles, with one hand holding the top of the towel and the other resting on her hip.

As she began to peel the towel away, letting pieces of her breast come into view, all thoughts of trepidation vanished, to be replaced by pure lust. She unfurled the towel from around her but still holding it over her nipples where I could see only the outline of her body. She squinted her eyes at me and turned a cheek as if casting a spell, then squished her lips together and let the towel fall to the bed, as she extended her arms out, displaying herself.

Not a hair, blemish, or tan line anywhere on her body, the image of every man's perfect female stood over me, teasing me, as my body responded primitively. My erection intensified, nervousness erupted in my chest, and rational thought ceased.

"Make me ready," she commanded.

She walked over my body until she stood over my face, her pussy dominating my view. Hers was gorgeous, with a smooth set of outer lips matching the color of her inner thighs, a thin set of inner lips with a slightly darker tone, around a barely visible glimpse of pink. Her clit poked out as she guided her hips down to my face.

Would I have ever turned down eating that pussy? Not in a million years, and I highly doubt any man ever did, even the chest-thumping drunks who claim they'd never eat bargirl pussy.

Her smile was that of a girlfriend, waiting for her man to pleasure her. Her eyes peered into my soul as her clit came to rest on my lower lip. I extended my tongue and contacted a dry vulva, the only dampness from the shower. I sucked her clit into my mouth as I extended my tongue into her, lubricating her for the action to follow.

As my saliva cleansed her, she rocked her hips, swallowing my nose on the furthest extension. The whole time, she gazed at me, as I gazed back. Was she enjoying it? The grin on her face hinted at amusement and the lack of moans or otherwise passionate mannerisms suggested no aphrodisia.

She reached her hand down to spread the top of her pussy lips and let her clit sit on my mouth, so I could focus on it. Her face turned stoic and her eyes squinted as she maintained her erotic stare. She slid her finger down and rubbed herself before backing off my face and resting her ass on my belly.

"Good job, babe," she said. "Do you have condom?"

Why do they ask me that?

I hadn't worn a condom since before Gib, and my monkey brain immediately searched for ways out of putting one on.

"No, I don't have, it's ok, I don't like."

She frowned and sighed. "Ok, just a moment."

She was going for her purse in the living room.

"Ok, ok, I have one," I said.

I reached over to the nightstand and produced a thin Trojan. No way was I going to experience her with one of those Chinese truck tires.

"Bad Boy!" she yelled.

My ploy didn't seem to irritate her, in fact, she giggled as she grabbed the condom from me. All par for the course in her line of work, I suppose.

Never asking me to do a thing, she rolled the condom on and moved to straddle me.

Again, with that seductive look into my eyes, she arched her back and dropped her hips, engulfing me in one motion.

Placing one hand on my chest to assist her leverage, she slid the other through the side of my hair, while I submitted to her hypnotic allure. She began to grind on me as if she knew the motion that was the fastest path to climax. Two minutes of her tight thighs slapping against my hips was all it took.

As I filled the condom, she relaxed her elbows on my chest and kissed my lower lip playfully. I wrapped my arms around her shoulder blades, feeling the touch of her desirable body press into me. She nibbled on my neck and giggled.

"You very good."

Without a clue as to what had just happened, I laid there holding her until my dick became flaccid. Was it purely her beauty or was it something more, something deeper within her? I was in a trance the whole time, still attempting to snap myself out of it, as if I was 16 and had entered a girl for the first time.

"Ok," she said, and patted me on the chest.

I released her and watched her bound off to the bathroom. *Oh, don't worry, I'll take care of the condom.*

Fulfilled, and yet so totally unsatisfied, I cleaned myself up and mused about the cruelty of passion. Porn and Gib, both of whom would never have left my side, compared to this cold-hearted whore, who seduced me like a chump and jumped off to rid herself of me as fast as she could. *Or did she?*

I stood in the door of my bedroom still naked as she exited the bathroom fully clothed and strode to her purse, to begin putting her things away. I sighed at the nature of the world. This girl was so out of my league that the turn of her head with the interested smile shocked me as much as the next words she uttered.

"You're nice, are you sure you don't want me to stay?" she asked.

No! Please just leave you bloodsucker!

A half-hour later, and 3,000 baht poorer, I approached the Walking Street marquee from Beach Road to meet Nok after sending her to the club to pay the long-time barfine. As I approached, I watched her practically dodging the steady stream of men filing onto the street, occasionally shaking her head at them while keeping a distance, as if she was being hunted.

Since she expected me to come from Second Road, I managed to sneak up on her as she moved far away from the mass. How else would I announce my presence? By pinching her ass of course.

Whap! If I had to guess, she'd performed that maneuver a few times, swinging her body around wildly connecting the back of her hand with my face.

"Oh my God! So sorry, honey!" she said.

She lunged forward to hug me while we both giggled. It was worth it.

"Were some guys after you?" I asked.

"Yes! Three man ask me go with them. Why you take so long?" she asked.

She had the spot already picked out for dinner. She led me through the Pattaya Beer Garden and to a wooden booth on the edge of the dock. I didn't even know it was a restaurant. Away from the bustle of the street with the hillside Pattaya sign looming over the bay and the shore lights from the hotels along Beach Road, I felt as if a romantic couple on a real date.

"Would you like to come to my home in Bangkok?" she asked.

"*Your* home?"

"Yes, I have for two years."

"It's your own home?" I asked.

"Yes."

"Not your family's home?" I asked.

"My mom lives there, but it's mine."

"How did you buy it? You have a loan?"

"My ex-boyfriend buy for me," she said.

"Your ex-boyfriend bought you a house? Where is he now?"

"He's with his new girlfriend."

Why was she telling me this so early? It's certainly not news to me that bargirls in Thailand manage to pilfer the bank accounts of men with more money than brains,

225

though the whole-house con usually takes a while. I pried the information out of her that she dated the man for less than a year, though it sounded as if he broke up with her... breaking her heart for another bargirl. I wondered if that was true, or if she suckered him for the house and then turned him loose once the cash flow dried up. The story influenced me, and was perhaps intentional, a clever way of informing me that if I desired her company, it was going to cost me.

My memory of the time is foggy, a product of the emotional impact of the last few days, combined with the astonishment of sitting across a table from such a gorgeous woman. But, to be sure, she already had her claws dug in me. I not only wanted to purchase her time, I wanted to purchase her affection, as if that would restore my satisfaction in the whole sex excursion, and validate my ego, for if I was capable of earning her adoration, even if through the means of lavishing her with gifts, no woman would ever seem out of reach.

In that dinner, of lobster and steak, cognac and San Mig, I learned a lot about Nok, or at least what she wanted me to believe about her. She aspired to work as a prostitute as a young teen, growing up in Bangkok and being witness to the life her older friends enjoyed. At 16, before she was old enough to work in the bars of Bangkok, she ran into a headhunter who brought her to Pattaya to a beer bar on Soi 6, where her young beauty and naivety was taken advantage of. I could only imagine those lucky guys finding such a treat on Soi 6, enjoying her body for a third the price I paid, and oblivious to her underage status.

It wasn't long before a 60-year-old sex tourist whisked her away to Singapore and attempted to wife her up. There, she got a real taste for luxury, and for what men were willing to give her, though he offered her all the support she would desire for her and her family, she couldn't abide the man's company and returned to Pattaya, but with a greater understanding of men. She had learned that men would do her bidding and it wasn't the quantity of customers where wealth was found in her job, but the quality.

After midnight, when we departed for the condo, I had connected with her. As she held my arm around her waist strolling toward Second Road, I felt I owned her, the same as I had owned Gib, I had merely upgraded.

At my condo, it felt the opposite, as if she was the one with ownership.

"Honey, give me massage, ok?" she asked. "That way I get horny."

From the first and every subsequent time, when Nok disrobed for me, she acted as though she was giving me the greatest gift a man could get. It may have been the way my jaw dropped but revealing her skin to the world was a choreographed work of art. Her movements were not the jerky pulls that most women execute to undress. She moved sensually, sliding each sleeve over her arm methodically as if a performance on its own. Her back was to me when she unclasped her shorts, before inching each side down over her hips separately in short bursts, leaving only her red t-backs hiding between her round cheeks. Before dropping the last article to her ankles, she'd peer around with the corner of her eye, the smirk on her face revealing the truth of her thoughts: every move was a cold calculation.

She glided onto the bed, ass in the air, teasing, tempting me, communicating that to have her, I must first oblige her. She laid flat and giggled, motioning with one hand to service her backside as instructed.

Giddy, I stripped naked and straddled her closed legs, my dick hardening as my balls scraped her ass. I placed my hands on her lower back and massaged the best I could, stealing a caress on her upper butt as I went.

"Mmm, my shoulders," she commanded.

For fifteen minutes, I massaged her upper back, each time I tried to go lower, she'd correct me.

"More please, my shoulders."

Just who was paying who here? Nevertheless, I continued the dutiful service, loosening up her back as she lay motionless with her eyes closed.

"Ok, you can massage my legs now," she said.

When permission came to move to her lower body, I was thankful for the extended time she required, it made it that much sweeter.

I was allowed all the feels I wanted on her ass, her hips moderately swirled as I massaged the back of her thighs, teasing between her legs. When newfound courage allowed me to invade the outer lips of her pussy, I discovered she was ready, her body submitting itself. I slid a finger between her lips to find her well lubricated.

She spread her legs and turned her head to eye me as I worked a finger inside, though I quickly learned that wasn't the service she desired. She extended an arm toward my head with an open hand as if to push my head down. No words were necessary.

I planted my forehead on her ass cheeks and engulfed her femininity. This time, her taste was enchanting, my primitive lust raging, basking in her estrogen.

Her hand on my head pressured me further, I arched my back, planted my nose in her asshole, ignoring the strained muscles in my neck. I pulled her vulva between my lips and ravaged her clit, finally extracting a moan of pleasure from her. She lifted her ass in the air, exposing herself more, a pull on my head nudging me upward. My tongue collided with her asshole, and her moan increased as I worked in a circular motion, only be thrust back to her clit a short time later.

The routine persisted for a good ten minutes, back and forth, lavishing her with oral service, until her climax neared, and she pulled me deep, communicating to focus rapidly on her clit. Her hand pumped my head as her moans turned to screams, her hips twitched violently, and she collapsed forward.

I darted to the dresser to grab a condom, covered my raging cock, and positioned myself between her legs as she lay still. Before I penetrated, her hand whipped backward, verifying the protection and reminding me she was still a professional. I finished myself off plowing her from behind as she relaxed motionless, eyes closed, and waiting for me to desist.

I rolled off, and she pulled the covers over her, without acknowledgment of my presence. I wanted something, a "good night," anything, even though a "you are so good" compliment like I'd received from so many other bargirls seemed too much to ask for.

"Tomorrow, can I take you to Central and buy you a dress?" I asked.

Da Fuck did I say?!

229

12

Hopeless Love

They say you can't buy love. I had put that cliché to the test.

After four days spent with Nok, I was 60,000 baht poorer ($2000USD). She was gone and I was laying in my bed, hungover and broken, staring at my phone hoping for her text.

It never came.

The eros I felt for Nok was crippling, a passion I had never felt in my entire 50 years. Normally, after freeing myself from a bargirl on the last two days of my vacation, I'd be eager for my final sexual experience. Not this time. My thoughts could not escape her.

Had she not been a prostitute, my fancy for her would have extended no further than a head-turn as she passed on the street, gawking at her beauty with the rest of the apes. On the Savannah, I would have been beaten away by the stronger males before ever caressing her skin.

In Pattaya, my money had bought a temporary entrance fee. She allowed me a taste of the world where I was the alpha male and she was the most sought-after female, but that fleeting experience could never satisfy me. The cavity in my chest burrowed deeper with each passing minute, as the realization I was nothing more than a customer sank in. She'd never text me, she'd never think of me. She might allow me to purchase more of her time, but I'd never have a place in her heart.

I would have spent more to try. I would have quit my job and tapped my retirement to stay with her. I wanted to visit her house, perhaps install a hot tub, some new TVs, buy her family some phones, or even a car. Nothing was out of the question for me. None of my possessions mattered, only her time mattered, and if I was more of a novice sex tourist, it might have turned out that way, but she made a grave error.

She had left that morning, hiding the joy from her face, after I decided to cut her loose. The night before, she'd spent hours texting "her sister." I knew she was texting a boyfriend, or a foreign customer, one that she had a fondness for. Besides that it was the middle of the night in Thailand and the middle of the day in Western counties, her face betrayed her delight as if finally speaking to a long lost love.

I was madly jealous.

The luxurious gifts, dinners at high-rise restaurants such as the Hilton Pattaya, speed boat outings, and endless massages and cunnilingus did not break the barrier to her heart. I knew I was nothing to her and I couldn't bear the thought of spending another day with her while she dwelled on another man somewhere in the world. *Jealousy over a prostitute... was I any different than Farang Bob?*

My understanding of the situation didn't stop me from hoping she'd text though. Perhaps she'd only want the money from another barfine, but I prayed her message would show some thoughts for me. So I lay there, a pit in my heart and my stomach burning, waiting for her text or for my flight home. Occasionally, I'd flip to pictures of Gib, a girl who gave me what I craved from Nok. A girl who in America I may have felt the same passion for if given the chance, but in Pattaya, where you could spend time with a girl of Nok's beauty, there was no place in a man's heart for one such as Gib.

Two days later, I boarded that A380, desperate to wipe the goddess's image from my memories.

If you made it this far, this book deserves a review! Even a single word and some stars will help its visibility on Amazon and motivate me to continue the saga, Bangkok is next! If you're worried about someone finding out, use a Pen Name, like I did!

I'm occasionally asked if my stories really happened. The answer to that is **yes**. The characters and events in this book happened. They didn't happen in the same order, I left out a lot, and I embellished, as all authors do. Names and places were of course changed.

I've kept in touch with many of the ladies I've met over the years in Pattaya. Most of them have found a man to take care of them. Do I have regrets that I'm not one of them? Sometimes, especially when I'm sitting alone in my cubicle, with nothing to look forward to after work but Netflix or a novel. But when the ticket is booked, and I'm counting the days until landing in an exotic destination, I'm always happy to be **solo**. Before you tie the knot, remember, you can make these trips until well into your 60s! Good luck in your travels!

N. Renly

Printed in Great Britain
by Amazon